Louis James Block

Dramatic Sketches and Poems

Louis James Block

Dramatic Sketches and Poems

ISBN/EAN: 9783337337414

Printed in Europe, USA, Canada, Australia, Japan

Cover: Foto ©Thomas Meinert / pixelio.de

More available books at **www.hansebooks.com**

DRAMATIC SKETCHES

AND

POEMS

BY

LOUIS J. BLOCK.

PHILADELPHIA:
J. B. LIPPINCOTT COMPANY.
1891.

TO MY FRIEND

DR. H. K. JONES

This Book

IS AFFECTIONATELY INSCRIBED.

CONTENTS.

DRAMATIC.

	PAGE
Exile—An Episode	11
Tantalus	83
Pygmalion	86
Hanging the Pictures	90

LYRICAL AND NARRATIVE.

Ad Poetam	95
The New Midas	96
The Feast of Roses	101
Ariadne	109
Actæon	111
Ithaca	114
A Dream	116
The Royal Questioner	118
Longing	127
Weaving	131
My Ship	135
Success	138
The Field	140
Wild Wind of the North	143
The Evening Star	145
The Drop	146
Snow-mist	147

CONTENTS.

	PAGE
The Cliff	148
The Rose	150
The Star	151
Resurgence	152
The New Day	155
Before Winter	159
Noon	162
A Summer Morning	164
The Inlet	166
The Voice of the Soul	168
The Sirens	170
Faith	172
The Quest	174
Forever	176
The Eternal Heights	177
Fate	178
A Thought	179
Solitude	180
Warning	182
Echo	183
Invitation	184
Premonition	185
A Platonic Hymn	186
Tuberose	191
A Sigh	193

SONNETS.

Suspiria	197
Sub-conscious	198
Sunrise in Winter	199

CONTENTS.

	PAGE
For Pictures. I.—War	200
II.—Peace	200
Progress	202
World-Slumber	203
Pandemos	204
Urania	206
The Soul speaks	208
The Intellect speaks	209
The Spirit speaks	210
Fulfilment	211
Dedication	212

DRAMATIC.

EXILE.

DRAMATIS PERSONÆ.

The Stranger.
Father.
Mother.
Ida. }
Alfred. } Two children.

Scene: The shore and waters of an inlet of the sea.

I.

The Stranger (*alone*).

Is there in the deed-world a deed, a way,
Worth doing or worth following? Is there aught
That can call out from spirit's secret deeps
The hopes, the longings, that lie sleeping there,
Until the hour, the time, ordained of God,
Touches them with light point of spear or dart,
And they leap forth in light? I cannot deem so.
The largest deeds of men are slender waves
Upon the sea's unmeasured stretch; a king
Sits high enthroned, and dim forgetfulness
Clothes him as with a robe; great love of men
Would set the crooked straight, and stem the stream

That flows to gulfs of death and shame, and turn
Its speed to where the happy fields are green,
But age on age the self-same tasks survive,
The work is still to do. So large man's soul,
That all the outer world is but a star
Upon its sky, and from its own deep might
Star after star appears—white lustrous births
From its unresting motions. All things are small,
All deeds but limited by things or deeds;
The sense of utter power, and might unswerved
From its clear end, resides not in the realm
Where souls appulse 'gainst souls, and the lame act
Halts far behind the wish; in thought alone
Is perfect freedom; even the seeming laws
Wherein all thought is bound, that wizard keen
Unmakes, and from the wide upheaval rears
Such domes as suit its myriad caprice.
The bitter code of good and ill, the feud
Wherein all pleasure dies, the rigorous choice
Compelling men to one strait way,—wherefore
Should the unconquered soul submit its head
To wear the yoke? In sooth there are two worlds;
I care not for that slavish bounded realm
Where there is work to do, and men meet men,
And strongest cords of relative despair
Encircle you; I see no cause to act;
I cast mine eyes upon the course of years
Even to the pale beginning. I see the world
Much like itself, bent double on its deeds,
And seeking the impossible,—to make
The world of work reflect the world of thought.
It is in vain, a futile opposition

To the essential framework of the world;
There are two worlds, a contrast sharp and dire,
And reconcilement cannot be. I, therefore,
Leave effort proved forerunner of defeat,
And with my thought am satisfied. I see
At will all splendor take on form and hue,
A pageantry of dreams pass through my soul,
Make joy for me past what the things can give;
For fantasy is more than all the world.
It is with thought that I am fallen in love;
I hate the sickly kissings, clasping hands,
The bitter bonds of love that lures us, love
As in the world misnamed, say, rather, lust
Or some such strain which is for beasts, not men.
But lo! I penetrate all mysteries,
I hold the keys, I watch how in my thought
Idea shapes idea, and the sphere
Rounds itself in the mighty thought of God.
I ponder the dark riddles of the sages,
I muse with the sweet poets, I forsake
The chill embrace of earth;—and this is best.
I shall withdraw me more and more, and reach
The peace which mystic faith has dreamed on, peace
Past understanding save to those strong souls
Who can renounce whatso the outer brings,
And live alone that hid internal life,
Which is the all in all, both each and all,
Oneness eterne o'erruling vast diverse,
Intellect pure in pure activity.

II.

ALFRED.

I wish I were at home; I hate the sea,
Where all day long you see no boys, and sand
Is all you have to play in.

IDA.

                But you swim,
And go out in the boat, and once you went
With father in a yacht, and stayed all night,
And caught great loads of fish.

ALFRED.

                        I want to be
Down in the town where all the men are gone,
And have the boys to play with, but out here
You only see the water—just naught to me—
And gather pebbles girl-like on the beach,
And swim but once a day—a mere half-hour.

IDA.

I like to see the waves roll far away,
And watch the wind make them look dark, and how
The little, clean, slim fish shoot here and there,
And the bright ripples break upon the shore.

ALFRED.

I understand that girls may like such things,
In which I see no fun. I never know
What makes you glad, except you want me near,
And often kiss me out of time.

IDA.

               Oh—oh—
You boys have no conceit. I think it time
For me to go back home.

ALFRED.

               No, no, you must not,
And leave me here alone. We can but talk,
There's nothing else to do, and then you know
One cannot talk with one's mere self.

IDA.

                     Quite well;
I sat the other day out in the wood
Alone for two long hours, and all the time
I talked with persons that seemed in my mind,
And they were beautiful.

ALFRED.

                You mean you thought;
You make my head ache like the school-master,
Who tells us we must think, and so be good;
But I am sure he never thinks, or he
Would hardly scold the wrong boy as he does.

IDA.

You are just dull; it was not thought at all,
It was not like addition, but a dream
Such as you have at night, save that you wake.

ALFRED.

And will you tell me what your dream was like?
I little understand you when you speak,

And say these curious things, but still I like it,
And my head sounds as though a bee shut up
Sang in my brain, and I knew what it said.

IDA.

But you must not break in and laugh;
That makes me cry; I love what my dreams show,
And you are cruel like most boys.

ALFRED.

       Nay, cease;
You know I never laugh at you; I laugh
Because the story makes me, and you cry
When most I love you; for somehow you seem
So good when you go on and talk.

IDA.

       Well, then,
I will begin. You know the wood I mean—
You cross the hill, and in the hollow there
The trees stand thickest, and all is so still,
You only hear the waters washing faint
And far away. The roses there grow wild,
And in one spot the thick, wild grape-vines grow,
And the sweet odorous roses climb high up,
And you can sit within a summer-house
The good God made.

ALFRED.

    I know the very place;
Where we went picnicking, and father said,
If he had money, he would buy the ground,
And build.

IDA.

   I sat there for awhile and sang,
And then I know not how, but this I saw—
The long green grasses swayed, and rose, and swayed,
And all the wild flowers I could see; I knew
That there was little wind, for the tall aspen
Scarce showed the silver of its trembling leaves.
So I grew still, and watched what I could see.

ALFRED.

And what was that? You take so long to tell
What I should say in half the time.

IDA.
         At last
Out from the spires of grass, and all the flowers,
I cannot tell you how, a fairy leapt,
And soon the air was changed, a golden gloam
Came in its stead, and on their swiftest wings
They flew and sought a level spot—just where
The mossy old stump stands. I saw them plain,
The fairies of the grass were long slim things,
With queer peaked faces, and long golden wings
They folded round them like a dress of light,
And when they sang, you heard a small soft sound
That was right sharp in sweetness; but the roses—
From them there came small lady-like sweet forms
That were all fire,—but not the fire that burns,—
A rosy gentle flame; they flew in curves,
And sang a song that makes me love you better;
But the buttercups would have been joy to you,
For they were stout, and clothed in shining gold,

And seemed to lord it everywhere so that
The violets, so thin you hardly saw them,
Nor knew them from the air, scampered away
When the gold tyrants came; but night would come
Before I told you all.

    ALFRED.
      What did they there?

    IDA.
I cannot tell; I heard their voices small,
And they flew round me so that—as, at night
When you put head beneath the coverlet,
You see the fire and color interweave—
Their forms of many hues blended and mixed
And fell apart, a shifting play of flames,
Red, blue, and gold, and all so full of glee
That now my heart is glad to think upon it.
I sat quite still, and tried to stop my breath,
Till I began to weep, and then I laughed,—
And at the sound, they vanished, one and all.

    ALFRED.
That is a pretty tale; you must have slept
And dreamed.
    IDA.
     If you go on as you do often,
I shall be sorry that I told you.

    ALFRED.
        You say
You saw, and were awake? Hard to believe;
Why do I never have such luck as you?

But then I often find things when I walk,
And you find nothing.

IDA.

Well, then, be content.

ALFRED.

But do you think the fairies really are,
And live within the grass and every flower?
Why then they die whenever flowers are plucked;
You cannot make me think that such things are,
I never saw one, and you only dreamed.

IDA.

You are too hard; why do you make me speak,
And tell you things, if you will treat me so?

ALFRED.

There, now, you cry, and yet I meant no harm.
Come, let me kiss you on your forehead white;
So, you smile through your tears. I understand
But little how you girls are made or think;
I saw you watch the other day awhile
The blood-red splashes left upon the sea
When the great sun went down; but father came
And brought the marbles, so I turned away;
But you and mother sat till the dull gray
Came on the sky, and the big ball of fire
Was gone, and you refused to play. Now say
What did you see?

IDA.

Why, you must look and learn;
The little waves seemed all to clap their hands

When a red ray went through them, and the clouds
Floated and swept to bathe them in the glow
As if they wished to die on the sun's breast;
And he shed forth his light intent to give
All that he had to make them glad, as I
Would do for you when you are kind to me.

Alfred.

Well, maybe I shall know when I am grown.
Now let us walk down to the beach, and play
At house-building, with me for architect,
And you shall order what you want; run, run.

Ida.

But I shall want a castle old, with towers
All clad with dark-green ivy-leaves, and windows
With diamond panes, besides a chapel grave
Where I can go alone, and softly pray.

Alfred.

Small use in that; you shall receive from me
A nobler gift,—a lofty brown-stone front,
With basement for the servants, and within
The walls well painted, and with mirrors tall
In parlor; nobody cares for castles now.

Ida.

It shall be as you wish; but see the waves,
How little sparks of silver fire bestud them,
And from the oars the fiery water falls,
And far away the distant blue shore lies
Like an unmoving mist.

ALFRED.
>Come on and play.
Here is the sand that reaches up the hill,
And we can build our houses as we list.
Come on and play,—what are you gazing at?

IDA.
It is the tall white stranger we saw before,
The silent man of sombre mien and garb,
With large, dark eyes that seemed to wish to weep,
And face white as mamma's sweet hand. You know
He stopped and watched us while we were at play,
Nor said a word, but seemed somehow so sad
That I felt I should like to speak, but then
He was so still and cold, I shook for fear.

ALFRED.
I would not mind; he will not trouble us;
We can, you know, hit him with some small stone
And then run straight for home, for it is time,
If we shall get our dinner waiting for us.

III.

THE STRANGER.
It cannot be; I dare not mar with change
The calm seclusion of my life,—the still
Unbroken sweep of waters guarding it.
My life has all the magical repose
Of some sweet island in a pale lagoon;
The ripples break upon the clear green waters,
The mainland lies afar enwrapped in mists,

The air is of a soft, mixed hue, not bright
As where the beast conglomerate, mankind,
The many-headed life that is but one,
Each puddled with the soul of each, doth dwell;
Even the sun veils here his rigorous splendors,
And paces with slower step the blue-stretched heavens;
The woods are peopled but with cool-eyed blooms
And slender well-poised ferns; and here and there
The white fire of the sudden springs, and birds
Whose voices are the sounds interfluous thoughts
Subtly project when several merge in one,
Conjoining rays in concord of one flame,
And the long grasses swaying in the wind.
Here all is peace and intellectual calm;
A mild self-centred spot which needs no commerce
With outward and debasing elements
To make its joyance; here I make my home
And meditate the boundless universe.
I see unfold the endless leaves of thought,
The petals rather of the great world-rose,
Until the inmost heart lies bare; I see
Within the multitudinous blood-red folds
The pygmy tribes of men; and History
Is as a silly tale told by the fireside
When the late night flares in last burst of gladness,
And soon deep rest shall hold the house; I see
The currents of the sap pass down and up,
The ceaseless potence of ideas great
That build and break, and at the hidden root
Great God himself, from whom all comes, who is
And is not the vast flower, and I am He
And All, when I ascend these easy heights.

But nothing foreign may intrude; disturb
The ambient atmosphere with sullen clouds
Born of the breath of unrespective soul,
And the high bliss is dead; disturb with check
Of contradiction Thought's unswerving flow,
And the bemired brown flood reflects no more
The picture of the sky. Here is my fear;
Into pure Contemplation's mystic round
I may not introduce the passions' whirl,
And that strange sentiment the fool man calls
Love; different by a world's wide interspace
From Love as known in Thought's dear Heaven. I
    pause;
Yet Beauty is this still realm's proper garb,
The robe external that expresses it,
And, while concealing, bares its secret heart;
And she—the lovely child—would be fit sign
Of its unbroken rest and splendid joy.
I cannot tell how she possesses me,
How my conception spheres her changing form,
As the round sky the centred earth; she flits
Into my every thought; her sweet smiles light
My deepest plunge of search; and science stern
Grows easy, and with prodigal outpour
Endows me with its secrets for her sake.
It cannot be that in my life's clear song
Her footsteps should make discord, or her voice
Not emphasize the surely-uttered words
That are the very truth of truth in forms
That are itself externalized. And yet—
Ah me—I fear lest I, precipitate
And led by sudden veer of impulse, throw

A hasty stone into my placid life,
And harm my safe release from human cares
With rippled thrills of feeling whose far end
Mine eyes discern not nor my thought. I pause;
When first I saw the grave small face, the eyes
Quite sad, but clear with some internal flame,
The lips closed in an ecstasy of dream,
I felt her as a sure inhabitant
Of those ideal plains where is Thought's home,
Or those miraculous vales high Fancy holds,
The varying image of the things that are.
Nay, I will not give way to fear; I dare
This deed, and quail not at the consequence.
She shall go with me; I will bear her home,
Engird her with most subtle influences,
And she will grow the white rose of the world,
The fairest lady in the worshipping lands,
A priestess in the virgin fane of Thought,
Iphigenia of these latter times,
The marvel of the ages, womanhood's queen,
Untouched of love or aught that can defile,
The lyre tuned to the planet's revolutions,
Star-taught to music, played upon by winds,
And voicing ocean's ancient mysteries.
Yea, I will go, and ask her of her friends,—
They dare not say me nay, I am sure fate,—
And if I must, my wealth will make me way,
For in the world of men I needs must use
Men's implements, although my heart abhors
Contact with these most foul necessities.
Yea, she will be to me my shaped expectance,
My life made clear to sight, thought clothed in form,

The apex of the pyramidal loveliness,
Like flame upclimbing skywards, which is my life.
I dare the high attempt, and build the realm
Which circles me, past outer might to break,
Wherein I breathe, clasped hand in hand with God!

IV.

ALFRED.

You do not build—what are you thinking of?

IDA.

I watch you, and it gives me more delight,
For I have no great skill of hand, and still
My walls and windows fall as fast as risen.

ALFRED.

This is your house,—four stories high, at least,
With rounded windows,—say how it pleases you;
See, I can make queer figures round the windows
And over the wide door—now, that looks right;
It shall be quite a palace when 'tis done.

IDA.

How do you make it all secure?

ALFRED.

                            I know not;
It stands just of itself, I think. Here are
Broad steps in front, and basement windows here;

I soon shall finish, and then give it you
In a long speech.

IDA.

           And I shall make reply,
And be all smiles, and say it is too much,
And nothing I have done deserves return,
And bow, and seem ashamed till all are gone,
When I can clap my hands and be plain glad.

ALFRED.

That will be fun—you girls are smart in speech;
I think you must have longer tongues than boys,
And pointed ones, for you are sharp at times,
And say what we can find no answer for.
How do you think a story more would look?

IDA.

Take care, or your frail sand-built house will fall;
You always go beyond the safety point,
And are impatient when your labors fail.

ALFRED.

Yet I will try, and you will sing the song
Mamma has taught you since we saw this place;
For somehow I can build best as you sing,
And raise my walls in concord with the sound,
For music is the only thing I know
Of the strange pranks you often tell me of
As passing in your brain not like my own.

Ida (*sings*).

I hear the waters call
    Unto me;
Into a dream I fall
    Of the sea;
I am borne in a slender boat
To where the moonset pallors float.

The white stars in the sky
    Glint and gleam;
I hear no voice nor cry,
    Save the stream
That is bearing me swiftly afar
Past earth's remotest bound and bar.

The moon rests on the sea,
    Silver white,
And shines in strangest glee,
    Subtly bright;
I pass to the viewless line
Where moon and trancèd sea combine.

I am the Lady Moon,
    And the sea,
I am the dim-toned tune—
    Utterly—
The waves and the flakes of light
Making send down the blue-roofed night.

I die into a dream
    Lighted dim,
I am the fitful stream
    Of the hymn
The Sea and the Moon and the Night
Fashion for joy and pure delight.

Alfred.

There now, 'tis done; did you bring down a doll?
She should walk in quite splendidly.

Ida.

                                        I know not;
Here is the little one you do not like.
You will not have her mount your marble steps?

Alfred.

No; but you said you meant to lose her soon,
Or give her to the girl lives next to us.

Ida.

And so I do; but I forgot last time
I saw her, and I left the homely doll
In this small apron-pocket unawares.

Alfred.

It does not matter. Now I think of it,
I mean to build a church with lofty spires,
And pointed windows, like the one we saw
In the great city,—made as though the stone
Into fine lace-work everywhere were carved.

Ida.

And I shall go sit by the silvered strand,
And think how each small boat bears thought of me;
For I shall give to every one a dream
That it will bear, and I shall seem to float
Out where the great waves toss and writhe, and winds

Have room to flutter out their widest skirts,
And freely tread the water's rippled floor.
I only would it were the wondrous night,
Set thick with stars, and overruled
By the sweet lady moon.

Alfred.

                     No, you must stay;
I cannot build alone, for if you sit,
And look on while I work, I can do better,
And my walls surelier rise. Now if you try,
You can make buildings too, old castles quaint,
With rounded peakéd towers, or chapels small
For ladies grave to pray in.

Ida.

                     It is in vain;
My hands pull down, I cannot raise a wall.
But, see, the stranger comes—shall we run home,
Or go on with our play and mind him not?

Alfred.

Why, let him come, he will not look nor speak.

The Stranger.

There is she now at play; her sweet grave face
Not lighted by a smile, and her dear eyes
Abashed beneath the flower-like lids. The sun
Is glad to play with her gold hair, and make
A fluctuant aureole about her head.
How I delight to see her little hands
Flicker across the sand in white fair gleams,
And all her motions glad as grace itself!

The lips are parted and I hear low sounds—
No song—but some dear chaos of dim tones
That will in time take shape, and be a tune
Taught by God's angels; O sweet child, mine own,
It cannot be that aught save loveliness
Can bloom or be where thou art—beauty's soul,
And Heaven grown visible.   I have no fear,
I will go speak to her, although the boy
Perforce must bring the world into our speech,
And gloom across our realm of poetry,
Even as a mountain throws large shadows down
Where the small waves imprisoning fiery gold
Weave on the sea the miracle of the song
The day and wind and waters hold soul-hid,
Or as a steep and blossomless review
Frowns with deep shade upon a valley-poem,
Where the mild violets hide in pallid grass,
Where the white foam of rivulets blooms to die,
And all the winds are sweet with endless spring.

IDA.

Oh, brother, he is coming—let us go;
I fear that he will speak, and my heart beats
And chokes my breath.   I feel afraid and strange;
I think his voice will be a wizard spell
To make me do what I desire not—come!
We shall return—pray, come—I dare not move
Save you are near to help.

ALFRED.

                A little while
And we must start—for you know dinner waits;

Meanwhile I purpose finishing my church.
You are just foolish—let him say his say—
We need not answer, and he will pass on.
I am not troubled.

IDA.

   Nay, but he will speak,
And his voice cold as are his far-off eyes,
And his words strange as are his pale calm lips
Make me afraid or ere I hear. I know
His deeds and speech will be as fair as friendship,
Yet I would rather pass him by.

THE STRANGER.

     A house—
And nearly reared a stately church—dear boy,
Your hands are skilful past the common wont.
Where learned you this fair craft? Your sister here
Gives help with her sweet smile—she labors not—
Or speaks encouragement with subtle words
You are most glad to hear. Were I at home
I might be aid in your exploits of art.

ALFRED.

I care not for your aid.

THE STRANGER.

    But if you knew—
For I have books wherein tall dwellings stand,
Made in times past, and wonderful to see,
White temples shining in the midnoon sun
On heights that overlook the fair green fields,

Old palaces made splendid for great kings,
And ivy-clothéd ruins, hoar and quaint.

ALFRED.

I care not for old books, and reading hard
For wits like mine to understand.

THE STRANGER.
                                      His rudeness
Might make me pause—my voice clings to my throat,
And all my body shakes—'tis always so
When I adventure in the outer world,
Nor dwell secure my soul within. Too late;
I cannot now refrain who see her face,
White and lustrous as the one star of eve.
'Tis not my wish that you should read my book—
These are fine pictures fit for eyes like yours
Or your sweet sister's. If I brought my book
Would you look on it with me?

IDA.
                No.

ALFRED.
                            I think
My sister wishes not to speak with you;
For you are strange, and not like men we know.

THE STRANGER.

And yet I have desire to hear her voice.
She is not unlike a dear girl of mine
About her age, and slender-shaped as she,
Whom I saw placed in the cold, rain-wet grave,

And I was left to weep. Dear gold-haired child,
How would it please to come with me?—my home
Is in the far-off hills; it stands alone
In a vast garden, where the largest flowers
Blossom and burn the summer through, and winds
Blow languid with the weight of perfumes, where
Under deep trees the winding pathways lead
To lakes set like clear stars on the green sky
Of grassy miles, where in the solemn shades
Of old oak woods the hours are filled with dreams,
And if you shut the outer sense you hear
The music that is played in fairy-land.
How would you like to go, and be mine own,
A daughter in my house of golden spells,
Where all you wished would speed from out your soul,
Swift changed to flowers for you to hold in hand,
Where you should be a queen—what say you, child?

Ida.

Oh, brother, it is time; I shake for fear—
He means to take me with him—give your hand.

Alfred.

And I shall find a stone to throw at him;
But then he talks like you; my brain turns round
With wondering what he means.

The Stranger.

                                    You are not going?
Let us walk by the sea, and watch the waves,
And see the fish gleam through the waters clear;
And I have tales to tell you of the past,—

The days when fairies hunted in the grass
On chargers small as are the gold-green flies
That star the air with fire; or of the days
When knights clad all in steel set thick with gold
Traversed the land to break enchanters' spells,
And free the long-haired damsels kept in chains
And held in noisome dungeons, where the light
Poured not its opulence of gifts; or days
When dryads shy lurked in the rustling woods,
And hoofèd satyrs danced when old Pan played,
And through the roads of stars Diana sped,
The maiden-goddess white as are your thoughts,
My small Diana come to earth again.

Alfred.

The stone just grazed him, we must turn and run,
He might strike with that slender stick of his.
I feel much grieved I did not hurt him sore,
But my hand trembled, and I could not throw.

Ida.

Now let us speed as quickly as we may;
I would not have you hurt him, but I fear,
And shall be glad to be at home again.

Alfred.

Turn now and look—how his eyes follow us.

Ida.

How white he is, and seems most deeply sad!
If I but had more heart, I would go back,
And speak to him, and beg him not to mind,

And listen to one story, but I shiver so
I must get home; come, brother, hasten on.

V.

The Stranger.

I stand here trembling like a feeble boy,
As if the sweep of some experience,
Soul-shattering, and remoulding life in forms
That make the aspect of the universe
A face of deeper truth, had come upon me,
Had torn through all my body's space, and left
Me changed and alien to my former self.
My heart beats, and my breath comes quick and loud,
I seem to sigh, not breathe; it is all vain;
I dare not enter those forbidden haunts
Where general man builds homes, plies myriad tasks,
Plays games with vari-colored loves, seeks ends
Of transient glow, and on the fitful breaths
Of friends erects frail dwellings mutable.
I am so lightly swung on tenuous nerves,
That a faint wind that lifts no gossamer
In land of most men's lives, shakes me with shock
Of earthquake, and confuses me with fear
Lest my demesne in earth's firm-poised extent
Will fall to dust, and past the reach of things
Be cast to realm of nothingness, and fall
Within annihilation's grasp. I fear
The converse where swift wit is masterful,
I tremble when I see the gathering crowd
Prepare to darken day with their weak speech;
Not fear, lest their base acts can work me harm,

Or futile thoughts bemire my statued calm,
But natural shrinking from their lower mind,
And innate horror of the stagnant pools
Wherein they dwell of thought and slavish hope;
Wherefore I needs must pause; how if I bind
These freest limbs with hateful bondages,
Break the blue-skied and sweet-aired leisure's calm
Under whose roof I pass mild days with clouds,
Strange loves and curious hates will quickly frame—
For these two are yoke-fellows, never one
Appears unless the other walks full near.
If she would give up all her simple past,
Leave all behind that made her life before,
Wash from her memory what but brings it pain,
That on the white expanse of her large soul
I might write splendid thoughts of Heaven and God,
Bring her where shine the bright and changeless stars,
That in her lucid eyes their shapes might dwell,
That in her lucid mind the fiery spiritual sun
Of high philosophy might rise and burn,
And she would dwell in domes not built of hands,
But every stone a thought miraculous,
Each window a clear glass to deepest truth,
Each chamber some great dream of poet-sage,
Each door give access to the unsearched fields
Where bloom the eternal flowers that God still frames
Lest man his creature make an end of things,
And Niobe-wise proclaim his larger scope,
And dare rail at his power! I tread the verge;
It may not be—the outer clamor sounds—
It may not be; the brother is a storm
Whose wrath makes dark the time I dream upon,

And in the mother's eyes no doubt are tears—
It may not be; for I cannot evoke
From slumber in a mother's deepmost heart
Sorrow and longing and their myriad tribes.
Pain is but of the world; and I would not
Stain my cleansed hands with implements of woe;
Even to think thereon makes my heart beat,
And the unuséd tears to flow; I feel
That at this price I purchased noble peace—
The world and its most clamorous dignities,
Its golden pomps, its strong ambition's steeps,
Its whirlwinds of applause that seize the soul
And bear it to a realm of passioned joy,
Its friendships that have something sweet and good,
Its love that builds an isle of maddest bliss,
Mingling the soul and frame in keen delight
Of frozen fire, as if the summer's heat
Should mix—a miracle—with winter's chill,
And from their clasp leaped forth an ecstasy
That joined their several joys—all these—all these—
I threw away as of small price or cost
That I might have ideal calm, the peace
Which is akin to God's, wherein swift dreams
Pursue great thoughts, and I am still at one
With the deep life that is in all that is.
Nay—I give her up; to breed great woe
In a dear mother's heart, a little one
To bear from the fireside where smiles and talk
Illumine more than the quick-leaping flames,
And ere the lights are set the shadows' play
Is weird and mutable as fancy's games
In children's hearts, is too hard task for me.

I consecrate anew life's brief remains
To clearest meditation, and those thoughts
That hold the universe in scope, to hopes
That lift humanity aloft to heights
Where the faint noise of struggle, grief, and pain
Shall change to music as things over-lived;
For in the memory's twilight, one by one,
The stars of long-done deeds arise, and grief
Outworn flames with a steady silver fire,
Till the vast night of the unforgotten past
Engirds with solemn splendor. I consecrate,
I consecrate, O God, my years to thee;
She is most fair, and I would fain see glow
The fire of grandest truths in her pure eyes;
But all this may not be, and I return
To my used solitude; to silent books
Wherein I pour my soul, and recreate
The minds majestic that upbore the world,
The imperial intellects that swerved time's course,
The living wills that were the seeds of acts
That will not end save with the end of things.

VI.

IDA.

Here let us rest awhile; I can no more,
And we are surely past his reach.

ALFRED.

                              You shake,
And you are white, and though you do not weep,
Your eyes seem as of one whose tears must flow.

IDA.

I cannot weep although I would ; I feel
Quite strange ; was there such cause for us to fear?

ALFRED.

I do not think it ; I had stood my ground,
But 'twas through you I acted as if need were
To fight him off; now that I think on it,
You were quite foolish, as you often are,
And with you near I do beyond my will
Things I should not attempt alone.

IDA.

                              Oh, brother,
You must not talk so ; ah, I weep at last ;
Yet you are right as I so frequent find you.
My heart is sad when I fall on to think
How my weak fears broke in on several joys ;
How white he seemed, and his voice shook alway
As if to speak were hard ; if we had gone
Along the shore, and heard him tell his tales,
It had been better ; yet I cannot tell
How some great dread took hold of me ; I think
If he should come again, I should repeat
What now I grieve at, having done.

ALFRED.

                              Well—well—
It matters not, sweet sister, let us on.

IDA.

We are not far from home; we need not run,
And when we gain the path that rounds the hill,
The house will be in sight and our way clear.

ALFRED.

See, sister, how the grass is full of color,
Low-drooping blossoms, and the snap-dragon,
And pale pink flowers I know not how to name.

IDA.

We can rest here awhile; you do not deem
That he will follow—I am yet afraid.

ALFRED.

Here is a smooth white stone, where you can sit,
And the thick-leavéd tree makes pleasant shade.
He will not come, and we are so near home
That they would know our cries if trouble rose.

IDA.

'Tis so, indeed, and while we rest us here,
You can cull perfect flowers, and clover leaves,
And the long grass with delicate-woven top,
And I will bind them in a sweet bouquet
For mother; for you bear in mind she said
That wild flowers made her dream of happy days,
And seemed more tender than the flowers of home,
That made your heart beat, but these gentle blooms
Brought back the times when she was young like you
And full of glee.

Alfred.

                It is a happy thought;
Meanwhile you can recover from your scare,
And need not frighten mother with a tale
Of terrible nothing, for he meant no harm,
And when I see him, I will speak to him,
And ask him of the pictures and the book.

Ida.

I shall not easily forget my fear.
But here is your bouquet, the flowers well set
In a green border, and the spires of grass
In feathery tufts o'erhanging with thin shades
The pallid colors under. Let us on.

Alfred.

We reach the turn of road, and mother stands
Looking down the tree-bordered length for us.
She answers my quick wave of hat—come, run.

Ida.

No, I must walk; I am all tired and hot,
And now I am to tell, my cheeks burn red,
And my strange fear renews.

Alfred.

                      You need not speak;
I will relate the startling thing for you,
As you are wont to make the little great,
And out of a slim trifle weave a tale
That frightens mother, makes her white.

IDA.
> No, no,
You cannot tell, for I have more to say
Than you know of.

MOTHER.
> You have been very long.
Three times or more I stood at door to gaze,
And wondered what detained my little ones.
But you remembered me—thanks for the flowers.

IDA.
Oh, dear mamma!

MOTHER.
> What ails my little girl?
Have you been running, for you seem quite tired,
And shake as if much effort had unnerved,
Or set you trembling like a slender branch
A bird has leaped from?

ALFRED.
> Let me tell the tale;
I shall not take so long, for going straight
I reach the end far quicker.

IDA.
> Oh, mamma,
I am not tired, but he so frightened me,
That I must weep; and yet I feel deep shame;
For he was kind, and meant no harm; I spoiled
His wished enjoyment, and kind brother's too.

Mother.

My child, you need not weep; I kiss your cheek,
And in my arms fear may not find a place.
My little one, come, ease yourself, be calm;
So, lay your head against me; tell me now
Who *he* may be, and what adventure strange
Stirred in your heart such fear.

Ida.

     I am ashamed;
He was quite good, and brother wished to stay.

Alfred.

You need not speak; we met the black-clothed man,
I told you how he gazed two days ago.
He came while we were both absorbed in play,
Looked on awhile with large surprisèd eyes,
Then praised my houses, spoke of picture-books,
But sister felt such fear, we ran away.

Ida.

There is much more; he spoke of his far home,
And all the splendors it enshrined, and asked,
Would I not go with him? It is most strange,
But I felt quite as though I must obey;
I tremble now to think of it.

Mother.

     Dearest,
He spoke but as one might in jest, no doubt;
You cannot think he meant it otherwise.

Remember that but just a day ago
The friend you love so used the self-same words,
And you laughed as you clung to me.

ALFRED.

                                                 But I,
Dear mother, threw a stone at him that hit;
I do not deem it hurt—would that it had!

IDA.

You are too rude by far.

MOTHER.

                                  Well, dry your eyes,
And now forget it all. You are at home,
And you shall go no more along the beach,
Unless some older friend companions you.
And yet my little girl must cease these fears,
And bear a stouter heart.

FATHER.

                                  Delay not more,
Go in, the dinner waits the truants twain.

ALFRED.

Father, was I far wrong because I threw?

FATHER.

We shall not speak about it further now;
Go in, and at more leisure we can talk,
And penetrate the matter through and through,
Although remember still to play the part

Of a courageous brother apt to help.—
What shall be done with our sweet sensitive plant
That shuts when the breeze freshens? She was not
    made
For earth, but some ideal virginal realm,
Some land of solid dream, whose air is song,
And all whose life is simple peace and joy.
Perchance she came from thence to light our home,
As a white lily lights the forest's gloom,
Or through a rent of cloud a mild star shines,
And saves the night from storm. Alas for us,
If we have not the power of wisest love
To bind her to us here.

MOTHER.

                Speak not such thoughts;
They clothe a real fear in garb fantastic,
A fear I shrink to put in words or form.
I drive it to some far recess of mind,
And lull it with the melodies of hope,
Till it falls on light sleep. I cannot think
Of aught befalling our most gentle child
Save life's divinest ministerings.

FATHER.

                Forgive
If I have roused the woe you sang asleep.
I would that life withheld not high success,
That ever flies my best-adjusted aim.
For her dear sake I would have liberal wealth,
And that fine grasp of possibilities
That should assure to sight her lightest wish;

For she is fashioned in so noble mould
That no result of pride or baneful scorn
Could yet ensue upon her gaining all
That widest life can give.

MOTHER.

      The same sad chord;
I bid you now again renounce the strain.
She will have love to wait upon her steps,
And make the frowning face of time relax,
And change to smiles; surely that is enough.
In your strong hands and gentle as great strength's,
She will be safe, and grow a human flower,
That makes the space she dwells in full of joy.

FATHER.

If it prove so, it will not be to me
The high result is due. A sudden thought;
'Tis he, indeed.

MOTHER.

    You reproduce the child
In obscure hints of *he*. You speak of whom?

FATHER.

You know the sad recluse, the scholar mild,
Who dwells in outskirts of our busy town,
I saw him yestermorn in reverie
Pacing the beach, and wrapt in mystic dreams,
Scarce like a denizen of our world.

MOTHER.

      Ah, so!
I do not wonder at the child's affright;

His cold calm eyes, and utter-abstract mien,
Fill me with dread when at rare times I go
Past the great garden which the summer makes
A gem miraculous set upon the ring
Of our dear town.

Father.

          I cannot longer doubt,
He is the man, and we must have great care
Of our dear girl's play on the beach; her frame
Can bear but ill these gusts of feeling strong
That are beyond the wont of her bright youth.

VII.

The Stranger.

Here let me rest; no shore is now in sight
Save as on either side a faint blue line.
No boat but mine pursued by the white foam
Cleaves the gray waters; I will ship my oars,
And let the boat drift with the wind and current.
The silence is so deep that I can hear
As 'twere the sound of time as it fleets by,
The flow of that unseen and mightier ocean,
Whereon the barks of states and lives and times
Have been borne forth to death or sure decay.
Beneath its voiceless waves the wrecks are hid
Of hopes that oversoared its blue of sky,
And stood at gaze on God; of joys that crushed
The whole world as clear grapes upon the lip,
And drank intoxication of red wine
That made the soul, large as the universe,

Scorn the earth's round as a child's outgrown toy;
Of fierce disdain upon whose lofty ridge
Stood poised the soul in utter rectitude,
And showed the world where Right shone as a sun.
Upon this dizzy verge the Present stands;
I look adown the abyss, and see the whirl
Of the fast-vanishing Past, and mightiest thrones
Of noblest virtues, images of dreams
Supernal, and extremest heights of thought,
Flicker like stars across that nether sky,
Burn, bicker, flash, are seen no more forever;
And like a mist wherein the strong winds strive,
The Future rolls before, and underfoot
Solidifies, while all that is, is not,
Down-sunken in the gulf that waits for all.
O soul, that holdest in thy reach of thought
Time with its vast contents, and teeming space,
Thou need'st not tremble while the spectacle
Furls and unfurls, appears, appeareth not,—
The immutable mutation, changeless change,
That in its variability hath rest.
Is there no permanent? no higher thought
Wherein the riddle answers its own quest?
Nay, here are visions born of corporal eye,
Fair shapes the senses build and break, a world
That is but as the gazer looks upon 't.
Eternity is that concentring point
Wherein all rays of being merge, the Now
Born of the Past, and holding the To-Come
As seed for ripening; there, O soul, dwell thou;
Nay, dwell not, rather be thou that great thought,
And so become the circling Universe,

Transfuse the flow of things with thine own self,
And win essential immortality.
The light breaks through the clouds with this deep thought,
As though the outer symbolled in great joy
The rapture of discovery; 'tis well;
As on my soul floods the wide light of truth,
So flood, O sun, thy realm with radiancy.
It is a fair new day; I call it fair,
Although the sombre gray of possible rain
Pervades the air, and the impetuous sun
Is shorn of half his glory or ere it falls.
Look to the hollow globe of sky—how fair!
In mass on mass of softest pearly tint,
And narrowing circles to the central point,
The mountainous clouds climb the steep curve of sky;
See there the space of unveiled central blue,
Intense in brightness past the power of words,
The fleece-like clouds in sweetly-broken shreds
Environing it; the waters lie below,
A rippled floor of sober shine; ah me,
The wondrous air, most clear, most full of glow,
And every cloud and every fitful wave
Is dowered with perfect color; so I drift
Through the pale Paradise of simple Truth.
I mind me of the old philosopher
Who saw the pure Ideas in their dance,
Prefiguring the worlds, and, rapt in dreams,
Beheld the plains whereon the assembled souls
Choose lives to languish through beneath the moon.
Can it then be that on the upper air,
As on the ocean's waves, green shores advance,

And beings dwell whose drink is some fine ether,
Who scorn our gross embodiment, the garb
Wherein our souls are prisoned, and who are
Companions for the often-visiting Gods?
I poise me on yon cloud and dare to dream
How life is shaped in that cool, placid realm,
A life of thought, clear, passionless, remote,
Unvexed by winds of fierce emotion, calm,
And resolute to pierce the core of things,
Bathed in the nearer sunlight, unbestained
With exhalations of our atmosphere.
But lo! I dream in sooth; not of the cloud
Is the pure vigor that has rapt my thought,
Not based on mists that from earth's ocean come,
And are but outwalls of its sullen realm;
Above the height of air and concave sky
That limits mind of terrene men, I soar
Into the thinner ether, which to breathe
Slays the dull body's weight, and robes the soul
In nudity of clear expression, form
That is Idea's self; but see, I drift
Close to the shore, and the sun's burnished rays
Clothe with light fierce as many-flashing steel
A single spot in the encincturing landscape,
All else being wrapped in shadow pale, subdued;
Like gems the sweetly-shapen trees drink in
And then reflect the partial splendor; a path
Winds through the gold-green arch of greeting trees,
And at the avenue's end a white small house,
And children at their play. It cannot be!
And yet the thrill of pleasure that unmans me
Cannot deceive! That purpose will not down!

And now I hear her laugh; it is the voice,
And as she moves, I see the childish grace
That has a charm such as a queen of elves
Might hold her subjects with; I do not err.
She penetrates by mystic accident
My solitude; alas! I hoped to tear
My roots of life out from the alien soil
They deeply clung to, dreams where she was queen.
Yet must I be a slave to whim and hope,
Be fettered by desire for earthly good,
Care for some waif of rude humanity,
Be tossed at will on waves of bitter love?
But I must think aright; the experiment
Is worth endeavor; I should make the girl
The pearl, the crown of womanhood; all Time
Her hand should wear as some slight ornament
That emphasizes beauty; secret lore
From the unfathomed Orient's store, and grasp
Of Nature that makes her obey the will,
With those high truths the sages hid in myth
Lest the profane should read, I give for dower;
I may not yield; I will resume the search,
And bear my bird unto my eager hearth,
Not so that she will dwell there sad and caged,
But that her song, grown strong with justest use
(The bounds of her sweet home being overpassed,
And youth's much need of wisdom's guidance done),
Will fill the reaches of the world's wide wood
With more than native fire of song, and rapture
Wherein the soul finds her primeval peace.
A joy, a fury seizes me, a bliss
That has not torn me since my vanished youth,

Since the fierce days when in the whirl of life
I plunged as a strong swimmer in the waves
Whose reckless foam burns gold in the high sun.
I swiftly seek the shore, I cannot fail,
It is a work set for me by the years.
Unto this height I clomb from whence all things
Are but slight elements in the vast view,
The oversight that merges in a point
The multitudinous universe, that has
The All engrasped, of knowledge absolute
The peak and summit; hither my soul has flown,
That it might ope the doors of some deep mind,
Might pierce the darkness of intelligence
That glooms it round, and, having shown the truth,
Arm it for fight with men—my task, indeed,
Save for my feeble flesh, and halting breath—
And so my world-work will be well fulfilled.
My little prophetess, your melodies
Will pierce the slumberous ears of the old world,
Awake the time to knowledge of high truth,
Give wings to cruel-fettered Liberty;
For I shall die, but you will be my soul,
To shed my thoughts as leaves upon the winds,
As rays of light upon the air, or rain
From highest clouds upon the thirsty fields,
My little singer, whose deep thought am I!

VIII.

IDA.

Stir not, brother, but watch the brown small bird
That stands here in the grass; note his clear eye,

See how he moves his lissome neck; and now
He flits upon the tree's swayed branch, and gazes;
There, he is gone, a brown speck in the air,
Cleaving his way as the slim fish the sea.

Alfred.

Father, when shall we go into the town?
Is it your wish to have the boat made ready?

Father.

It is not time; I wish to stay awhile,
My book has yet some pages to be read,
And I am here so pleased with the cool peace
That I shall hardly care to go.

Alfred.
     Well, then,
May I go out alone?

Mother.
      Pray, be content,
And sister soon shall go with you.

Alfred.
       This tires me;
You all have books, or Ida watches birds,
Or, stretched upon the grass, looks at the flowers.
I know not whither I may turn.

Ida.
       Dear brother,
Look up into the sky. High overhead
The thick clouds seem asleep, but under them

Thin films, most white and pure, float on the wind,
And where the sunlight falls, they softly shine,
As if all through them flashed a sudden joy,
And they are lighted as a face with smiles.

Alfred.

It is a pretty sight; the large clouds break,
And the thin shreds float on, showing the sky's
Pale blue through their faint woof.

Ida.
       Come, play;
The little clouds will be our messengers,
And bear our thoughts away, what do you think?

Alfred.

A silly game; but as I needs must stay,
'Twill do to pass the time.

Mother.
       Now, that is sullen;
Besides the day grows hot, and on the water
The strong sun beats unhindered, save for the shades
The swift clouds throw.

Alfred.
      But in the boat 'tis cool;
For the large wind has play, and calms the heat.

Ida.

On with our game. I see a slender waif
Float on the wind like a white fairy skiff;
I bid it bear for me a beam of light

To fall upon a lady's finger-ring,
And call from sleep the fire and gold are there.

ALFRED.

I give that large white bark with back-blown pennon
A wind to hold, whence it will flutter loose
Against the small sail glittering far away,
That the swayed boat may skim the yielding waves
With speed to make one glad.

IDA.

      Mamma, you speak;
You send the dearest wishes, and 'tis joy
To have you mix with us in play.

MOTHER.

      I send
Upon that highest cloud a golden dream,
A dream that may come true, a dream of love,
That grows to bright reality—for whom?
For the pale stranger that you met and feared.

ALFRED.

Now, father, 'tis your turn.

FATHER.

      If I shall play,
I send upon that swiftest cloud a Thought,
A Truth, that it may poise above the head
Of the pale student, flash through his tossed brain,
Lighting the white transparent face with flame,
And making clear the mystery he pursued
For weary years with swift discovery.

ALFRED.

I see afar a cloud with wings outspread
Quite like a bird; I hang upon its neck,
My carrier-pigeon's neck, an unseen missive,
That all the boys may learn of the wide world,
How glad it is to feel the wind and spray
Dash on your face when out far on the sea.

IDA.

I see a cloud all fervent with the sun,
Washed with the light, and sailing slow afar;
Into that downy nest I set a bird,
The bird of a sweet song, that will be borne
Back to our home, and there abide for us,
Till in the winter time it melts in tone,
And our rapt thoughts are carried back again
To this sweet shore, to this faint-sounding sea,
To the fair rose-glen just beyond the house,
To those bright flakes of fire upon the deep.

ALFRED.

Upon that great white ball I place a statue,
King-like and crowned; let him compel the nations
To hold our land in reverence.

IDA.
                    On the verge,
Where the horizon gray curves to the sea,
A thinnest vapor speeds; 'tis scarce a cloud,
And more like light slow-hardening; in its woof
I mix I know not what, a drop of soul,

That out of it a rain may fall on hearts
Fulfilled of pain, and they may quickly wake
As from a dream, and be mild-glad again.

Alfred.

I have enough; father, read us a tale,
From the old book you were so glad to find,
And much surprised at yesterday, of how
The king went hunting through the enchanted wood,
And found his lady changed into a vine.

Mother.

A happy thought; we all are just in mood
To hear; and those rich Oriental plays
Need to be read when we, in tune with nature,
Feel not abrupt the change from daily mind
To that sublimed and mystic consciousness.

Ida.

I sit upon the grass next to mamma;
It is as well as going in the boat.

Alfred.

'Twill do awhile; but I prefer to row,
And fight the wind, and cut right through the wave,
And know how strong I am.

Father.

     I have the place;
Shall I go o'er the part we read last time?

Mother.

A pleasant thought; but lo! a stranger stands
At the path's turn, and is at point to come.

Ida.

I must into the house; for it is he,
And I yet fear to meet him.

Alfred.

     What foolishness!
You said you would be braver, and you blench
The first time you are tried; I mean to stay
And hear him speak.

Father.

    No, children, get you in,
Or play in the green field behind the house;
We shall remain to build acquaintanceship.

Ida.

Come, brother, like the dear good boy you are;
I tremble when I see him. I will play
Any game that you like, come but with me.

The Stranger.

Your pardon if my suddenness offend,
And yet I deemed a fellow-townsman's right
Would fail not recognition.

Mother.

     You are welcome,
Pray you be seated; it is a pleasant thing

To meet away from home co-dwellers there;
It gives a sense of shattered lonesomeness,
And strips the place of strangeness.

The Stranger.

                      Yet strangeness surely
Can have slight hold where friendship pitches tent,
And family cheer sets up abiding place.

Father.

We freely bid you be that cheer's partaker,
And it will give us joy if we have power
To make you feel at home, so be there's need.

The Stranger.

You make me welcome to far better home,
I deem, than the outer can build up; in books,
Where greatest minds have reared an unseen world,
That is unto the things we see as soul,
A nobler dwelling is, more permanent,
More native to our best capacities.

Father.

Into that realm you will be worthy guide;
Report that lives on lips of wisest men
Holds little error, and we know to you
That realm's each flower-lit glade, each greenest nook
Of ancient wood, its smooth white sands of shore,
Stray slopes of blossom-joy in mountain folds,
High table-lands that rule the unmeasured fields,
All places of deep thought, and those hid founts
Of feeling where to drink opes the soul's eyes

To occultest mysteries, are as good friends:
We shall have joy to tread upon your steps.

The Stranger.

Yet vague repute still speaks with too large sound;
For through the yielding air the spoke word spreads,
And reaches ear with loud reverberation,
As a weak king enpanoplied in gold,
And wearing reflex glow of retinue,
May seem a very Cæsar.

Mother.

                    But the clear page
Whose magic letters hide a visible truth,
And are of might to fuse an alien soul
In noblest gladness, speaks more loud than fame
The sentences the latter utters.

The Stranger.

                          Be it so:
I dare belie not the deep work of years;
For I have trodden many paths of thought,
Pursued to their far haunts evanishing truths,
Found ways to disentangle thinnest woofs
Of the arch-worker, spirit, gazed upon
The elements wherefrom his world is made,
And watched him at his labors till I knew
Some deepest secrets of his handicraft,
And took his tools, and furthered his results.
But 'tis not of myself I mean to speak,
Forgive the self-love of a lonely man,

Who joins too little converse with his kind
To mould his speech to their accredited fashion.

Mother.

It always is our valued privilege
To step aside from the accustomed ways,
And with great sages meditate the world,
Not in its semblance, marvellous deceit,
But as it is to the opened eye of soul,
That visions not this realm of sense and time,
But the essential whole which is the life,
And in whose self-recurrent pulse all things,
All times, all histories, all human thoughts,
Are points of fact wherefrom it ever builds
Its mighty fabric—nay, I speak but ill,
Not it, but He who is the Life of Life,
And Soul of Soul.

Father.

        Go not into those depths;
The young day laughs, the gray clouds break away,
The sun points to the sea, a wealth of smiles,
And gives command with sweetest tyranny
To yield to it our wondrous molten souls,
Breaking in luminous ripples of fleet joys,
And ever-changing gleams of lightsomeness.

The Stranger.

A trip in yonder boat were not amiss;
Out to the central bay, afar from land,
In places where the many rarely come,
And the wide loneliness of sea and sky

Engulfs you in its clearness; underneath
The fluent waters, overhead the viewless air,
Away from all solidity, the soul—
A joy past earthly words subtly to frame—
Convinced of its eternity, and freed,
Or glad-forgetful, of its body-chains,
The world and all that is a fixed mere point,
Whereon it bird-like is light-poised awhile.

Mother.

Your words bring to my mind the poet's words—
His of the fiery soul, whose home was air,
And whose deep heart was torn with this world's woes
That reddened his fierce song's absolving flow;
You know the verses well: "I love all waste
And solitary places, where we taste
The pleasure of believing what we see
Is boundless as we wish our souls to be."

Father.

That poet seems a favorite; strange to me,
For he is mainly read and loved of men.

The Stranger.

But in the realm of mind all severance dies,
There oneness dwells, no barren monotone,
But unit-life ensphering all diverse.
Surely in thought the man or woman dies,
And simple human reasserts itself.

Father.

I cry you mercy—for the noble day
Still bids me bathe in its circumfluous sea;

I would but breathe and be, so wonderful
The golden clearness governs me.

Mother.
     And I
Would give you thanks; I care not overmuch
For those diversities our crude life frames,
And dwell by preference on those subtle hints
Of inner calm in whose mild atmosphere
All storms, absorbed as 'twere into the sun,
Yield place to grander forces.

The Stranger.
     Hark! a laugh
Rings clear across the air—your child's, I doubt.

Father.
Our little girl's whom you perchance have seen.

The Stranger.
I met two children playing in the sand,
A strong, stout boy, of a courageous mien,
And masculine eye, that dared the total world,
Companioned by a golden-haired sweet girl,
On whose pure face pure dreams had left their glow,
In whose wide eyes sat an unspotted soul,
Looking in strangeness on this lower realm,
As troubled with some unacquaintanceship,
And yet at point to dower it with its love.

Mother.
Our children build a world within the world,
And we together are a spiritual isle,

Engirt by the wide sea of all mankind,
An individual happiness, indeed,
But drawing life from the universal soil.

The Stranger.

No doubt you have the secret; I have sought,
But cannot say, have found; I feel the feud;
In solitude the shapes of grandest thoughts
Float in pure light before mine inner eyes;
But on the rapture of high meditation
There supervenes a mighty loneliness;
And yet the world of men I shudder from,
And know not how to bear myself in it.

Father.

Perchance, love holds the key; forget oneself,
Bind life with other lives, and the wide sky
Is clear of clouds.

The Stranger.

          I deem your words are true;
I would bestow my wealth's large sovereignties
On others; the power I grasp, so vast, so strong,
I am not apt to wield; no doubt young hands,
Made strong by will suffused of truest thought,
Might take the full nihility of wealth,
And bare the eternal statue lurking there.

Mother.

What better use of wealth than personal grace
Wrought in the soul by studious hold of books,
And making beautiful the transient spot
Wherein we dwell? Think you not so with me?

The Stranger.

Experience answers no. I would have one—
A child—a soul unharmed with life as yet—
To whom might fall the dower of perfect freedom;
She should have space to grow as grows a flower,
Fed by each wind full-freighted with God's stores,
Bathed in the light of his unceasing suns,
Taking from earth the best it has to give.
It were a task to soothe the approach of age,
And rob grim death of terror. I should live
In my sweet pupil.
Father.
     For you not hard to find,
I deem.
Mother.
  A pure desire well worth success.

The Stranger.

You have a child—a lovely golden girl—
And I—I might confer great benefits on her;
I am alone—I have not friends—but much—
Much else you know of—you are townsman mine.

Father.

Your words are difficult to understand.
You cannot mean——
Mother.
    You speak of our bright girl?
You would have her? take her from mother's side?
I cannot listen longer—let me go.

Father.

Sweet wife, be calm ; here is some mystery ;
I am not clear in what is said, nor you ;
Explain yourself more fully, we would hear.

The Stranger.

Forgive—I cannot now—I will return.
I am so little used to converse—I will go—
Yet ponder you my words—it will be well.
She will be queen—nor of the world alone—
But reign in the white land of intellect,
A sovereign woman, marvel of her times,
A light to burn adown the dusky road
Along which move the ages newly risen,
A fire to inflame in all men's hearts to come
Fierce love of truth, and all that is the best,
Another virgin giving to these sad latter times
A spiritual birth of deepest thought and hope,
In whose unceasing current whoso bathes
Will be reborn in inmost soul—but lo !
I speak wild words, yet not words void of truth.
Forgive—consider all—for her behoof.
I will return.

Mother.

   He is not right in mind ;
I feel as I could weep—for him—for me—
I know not well. What meant his passioned words?
Tear from my side my little loving girl,
Who needs a mother's hand, a mother's heart,
Whose soul would flutter in his gilded cage
As some bird newly caught, pining for wood

And cool upbearing winds? I am not clear
I seize his sense.

FATHER.

Take peace unto yourself;
He has lived long alone, and knows not well
How men are linked together, hence his strangeness.
Pity for him I beg who has torn his roots
Out from the general soil, and so must bear
An alien's part within the unheeding world.

IX.

THE STRANGER.

Shall I succeed? The doubt obtrudes itself;
I have been wrong, and clearly see wherein.
Thought is not solitary, rather grows
From contact of all souls; you break the charm,
And enter Fancy's changeful realm, who hope
From thought's mere exercise to build up truth.
My little girl will be an avenue,
A flower-fringed way to lead my footsteps back;
I hear her laugh sound through my vacant rooms,
And the large house recovers life and soul,
Touched by her magic finger; as in the tale,
A myriad hopes and possibilities,
And many fair delights have fallen asleep
In the wide kingdom of my heart; and she,
My princess, wakens all in this changed version
Of fairy-lore remote. I cast off fear,
I throw aside the cold reserve of years,
I mix with the deep life of human kind;

I know their joys, I feel the wondrous thrills
Of ecstasy that are their common fare,
I stand no more aloof; is it not true
That feeling holds the All dissolved as pearl
The Egyptian queen drank off in ruby wine?
I face the twin infinities; lo! Thought,
Amid whose placid plains and silver streams
These many years my constant feet have gone;
Lo! Bliss, a sea on which I dare to float.
I see the sister hold the brother's hand,
And melt division of the bodily frame
In one sweet innocent joy; I see the child
Stand by its mother's knee, and in their eyes
Their souls are one; I see friend walk with friend,
And the mild stream of converse is themselves,
No more dissevered, but each mixed with each;
The husband holds his wife against his breast,
And in the rapture of their beating hearts,
Fair marriage of two souls is consummate.
And lo! the world of passion; shall I quake,
And shudder back when these fierce gates expand?
The lover scatters kisses on his mistress' lips,
As in the wood, which a dim stillness holds,
The rose-leaves fall upon the moist soft grass;
Vague thrills of fear and hope assail his breath,
And in a dream he swoons, wherein his queen
Is mystic mistress of the winds and streams,
And naught is but themselves; and e'en the depths
Of mad delights, where still the soul is torn
By gusts of joy and hate, I dare explore;
The goddess of all lovers, pale and wan,
I see within her caverned mount, and him,

The knight who bartered life and hope for her,
Who chose sad love in lieu of God's own bliss.
But now an end, I must no longer rave;
I dare not trust that she will walk beside me,
And if I fail, I give up all attempt.
The trouble comes, I sacrifice the higher,
Pure intellect, to what is of the lower born
Perchance, and on that way is certain death.
Oh, wretched that I cannot cling to one,
But must bewilder me with many aims.
It is not done, they will refuse, I think,
And I shall have again my waveless calm;
That were the best, perhaps;—what is the right?
Will theyforego to see her, hear her, love her?
Have I the right to tear from mother's side
The child, and be a double criminal?
Criminal—harsh word, nor yet devoid of truth.
Down with these fears! For once I am a man,
A doer in the endless whirl of things,
No passive looker-on; what comes will come!
Meanwhile I put forth utmost power of hand
To grasp the fruit has pleased my eager sense.
I will give over thought, the balancing
Of many points of view, adjustment nice
Of motives filmy as the woven air,
Or quickly-vanishing mist, unravelling
Of elements fine as outspread web of light,
That garments the bright sky, a chemistry
Of spirit or of dream; lo! I will act
And bathe me in the stream of consequence,
Whereby I shall be man past what has been,
Yea, be in truth the deed, the power of God!

X.

IDA.

But do you think that he will come again?

MOTHER.

I have a firm conviction that he will.

IDA.

Then brother may go with me to the beach?

ALFRED.

Not so; I wish to stay, and hear him talk.

FATHER.

Yes, you may stay; we shall not see him after,
And both may hear the words he speaks.

IDA.

                            Dear mother,
Close by your side I shall not be afraid.

ALFRED.

What kind of man is he?

FATHER.

                     He is a scholar,
Has traversed many lands, and noted much,
Has studied deepest books and gathered lore
That none but loftiest intellects dare pursue.
He is most subtile, and I more than deem
Has lost himself amid a maze of thoughts,

So that no more he has a grasp of life,
But floats as a stray leaf upon the flood,
Or bubble through the many-pathéd air.

ALFRED.

You say what I can get no meaning from.

FATHER.

Most true; I lost your question, dearest boy,
And merely thought aloud; a learnéd man,
And yet I cannot call him good.

ALFRED.

       He spoke
Of picture-books, of churches old and fair,
Of mansions wide and grand he meant to show me.

FATHER.

No doubt he might if so he felt inclined.

IDA.

But he is sad, and in my utmost fear
My heart weeps for him.

MOTHER.

      There spoke my little girl;
He more excites our pity than our dread.

FATHER.

You know we have not wealth; how if he came,
And sought to bear you to his noble home,
And bring to pass your every lightest wish?
For he has power.

IDA.

     I shake with sudden chill;
These words are not for me?

MOTHER.

        I hold you fast;
It is a jest, a trifle cruel.

IDA.

      Him?
Go forth with him, and leave you all behind?
Say, must I go? But I shall surely die.
Dear brother, come to me; what can it be?
I soon shall tremble at you, father dear.

ALFRED.

You shall not go so long as I am by;
They cannot tear you from me, so be still.

MOTHER.

Appease the child; you will forego her love,
And much I fear me 'twill be somewhat long
Before she loses memory of this shock.

FATHER.

Forgive, dear child; I cannot tell you why,
But somehow I felt bound to say the words.
You should be free, I would not force your choice,
Though filial love makes you our own. Enough;
You are too young to understand my purpose.

Mother.
Your words make me ashamed of my swift harshness.
But lo! the stranger comes.

The Stranger.
     I have returned.

Mother.
We welcome you again.

The Stranger.
      I would be plain,
And to my business pass at once.

Father.
     Business?

Mother.
Let him proceed.

The Stranger.
    To you I speak, sweet child;
I am a lonely man, and your clear smile
Is like the moon in life's sad night to me.
Tremble not so; for I shall bring you joy,
And you will speak but to achieve your will.

Ida.
I am most sorry for you.

The Stranger.
      Great gladness comes
When you are near; you will not flee again?

IDA.
Your sadness grieves me, but I know you not.

ALFRED.
You brought the picture-books you promised me?

THE STRANGER.
I do forget—and yet—not now—not now—
Hereafter I may send you them. Dear girl,
Stand by me here, and let me hold your hand.

IDA.
No—no—I would not leave my mother's side;
Here I am safe—and you—I know you not,
You are too strange.

FATHER.
          You spoke but now of business.

THE STRANGER.
I do recall myself; your pardon.
I shall mean no offence, but I would speak
With freedom, and make clear my long desire.

FATHER.
Speak without fear; it is my pleasure's wont,
I have no love for windings in and out.

THE STRANGER.
I have great wealth, this is no news to you;
I have small faith in that munificence
Which feeds its vanity by large bequests

To public charities; the donor's will
Is not expressible in perfect words,
And the keen law's interpretative skill
Brings manifold meanings from distinctest speech;
So the bequest is tortured from its end,
And waters fields quite alien from the hope.
I would bestow my gifts with lesser failure.

FATHER.

You well express my thought; to be dispenser
Of one's own bounties seems the wiser course.

THE STRANGER.

You pardon me, I would enrich your days,
And change the dull monotony of your life
To graceful interchange of pure delights,
And harnessing the courser, property,
To the swift car of your sweet family cheer,
Set you at freedom from material chains,
And leave the world to master as you wished.

FATHER.

Too large a gift, too slender toil for me;
Achievement is the best reward of work.
I should refuse the gift.

THE STRANGER.

            But hear me through:
I am a lonely man; I would find way
To sweet communion with my fellow-man.
The sense of glad society is long disused,
And of itself the blossom will not grow.

I must find other means, and with your help
I shall not fail in its resuscitation.

FATHER.

If I can serve you in so wise a wish,
'Twill give me joy.

THE STRANGER.

           You have a fairy child,—
Her hand shall guide me from my wilderness,
Shall starwise lead me from the labyrinth,
As in the ancient days the enamoured princess
Led the Athenian stranger to the light.

FATHER.

I pray you come at once to your sure point;
In this obscure of words no thought is clear,
And I must guess your purposes.

THE STRANGER.

                 Not guess;
We both shrink from the edge; then here it is.
This golden-haired fair child, this visible dream,
I would receive from you to bear her hence,
A daughter mine. The world shall be her toy,
She shall be queen of the world's intellect,
Upon the waves of fame her name shall float,
A ship to bear great truths to sundered lands,
All womanhood centred in her noble life
Shall vaunt itself to have borne such prodigy;
Upon the mountain-peaks of time shall burn
Her beacon-thoughts to rouse the sluggish nations;
What would you more? you cannot say me nay.

FATHER.

You deem the answer easy; will the child
Return at intervals to home and friends?
For these, I doubt, in light of grandiose aims
Might fade as night's most fiercely splendent stars
Die on the breast of the effulgent sun.

THE STRANGER.

Return to home and friends? strange speech to make;
What have these here to do?

MOTHER.

                        Have you a heart?
You tear a soul from all it holds most dear,
Sever as with a knife bonds red with blood,
Make a young life as cold and lone as yours,
Suppress the love that flows 'twixt mother and child,
And then you say these have here naught to do?

FATHER.

Dear wife, no more. My daughter, listen well:
You see this gentleman; he offers you
Wealth far beyond your wish—and I am poor—
All things that make life worth desire to live,
Fame, splendor, power to do mankind much service,
Far more than your young years can understand,
And I can give you but a dubious joy—
For I am poor—save that you will be girt
By purest love; now you are free to choose;
Will you go forth with him?

IDA.
                      I catch your sense;
Oh, mother, loosen not your grasp from mine;
I have no more to say.

ALFRED.
                      I hate you, sir;
If you come here again I shall be wroth,
And take sure means to do you some fell harm.

FATHER.
You have our answer, sir.

THE STRANGER.
                      I hear not well;
This looks like a refusal—folly dire!—
Shall I not have the child?

MOTHER.
                      I can no more;
I pray you leave us now in peace.

THE STRANGER.
                      No—no—
I yet am at dull loss; my brain turns round;
You cannot be so cruel, yield the child.
A mother's selfishness should here give way.

FATHER.
Enough; you seem not swift to apprehend;
Have you not thought how in our close-meshed life
The law prevails of cost and price? Know that

Not fully formed into our grasp is given
The thing we seek; out of hard sacrifice
As from some savage jaw 'tis ours to rend
What so we yet desire. You dare to ask
The sweetest gift of man's, nor reck the cost?
Go! mix with men, dispense your charities,
In some fair woman's eyes doubt not to see
The image of your aims reflected clear;
Then out of duties nobly done, and work
Beside your fellows, as God's visible chrism,
There will descend from Heaven your dear reward,
Your child, incarnate symbol of much toil,
And yielding up of self, your own, no fruit
Plucked from another's tree, and lacking taste
To soothe your hungered heart; you ask in vain
What is not right to give, and, being given,
Could bring but death to you and her.

The Stranger.

                              And yet
My thought is pure; you break my latest hope;
To see my intent in mirror of your words
Is horrible. Can I be lost so far?
I am not used so to mistake the right,
Yet you seem right; I am quite broken down;
Grant me the time to gain my surer calm.

Mother.

Take comfort; we are sad to give you pain.

Father.

These are grave depths of thought; it is not well
To deem oneself sufficient unto all.

In this dark mystery that we call life
The appulse of souls and things and deeds so close
Connects the each with all that disarray
Means exile; as the tree draws life from air,
Yet rooted in the soil has dwelling-place,
And perishes withdrawn from vital circle,
So there survives no deed save as with all
It mixes in the spiritual ebb and flow
That is the soul of this vast universe;
Thought abstract feeds upon itself, a phantasm,
It traverses all time and space, nor rests;
Life fills it with red blood, though yet I deem
Mere living is but brutishness and dirt;
In realm of pure Idea is the source
Of light, we walk in darkness otherwhere.

The Stranger.

The attempt is over. If I have given offence,
Forgive. I am recovered from disease;
There needed but this last experience
To render plain how that for men like me
The intellectual is the sole repose.

XI.

The Stranger.

I feel deep shame—I must regain my calm;
But I shall prove apt learner. Here is end;
True, I was wrong to hope acquaintanceship
With action's small dexterities a task
Requiring little time; the soul descends
With troubled steps into an alien region.

The wisdom offered me with free outpour
I long have found stale and unprofitable.
Men have their functions, and the thinker stern
Is not the least of creatures; but I feel shamed
At having touched that baser sphere, and known
Weak thrills of soft lascivious feeling stir
My heart bemired; some large and cleansing thought
Will rid me of these stains! In the clear stream
Of some great book I needs must bathe, perform
Some vast and expiatory toil of brain.
I scorn myself, the humiliation beats
Against my brows, and drains my veins of blood.
The truths they spake have only relevance
Where souls yet infantile perforce seek aid
From mutual stress, that subtle slavery
Whence highest man superb erects himself,
And being all, is freedom, his true self.
But I shall soon forget; these latest throes
Fall from me as the cool clear drops of rain
From burnished leaves amid the sober wood.
I am restored unto myself—and never hence
Shall I make wandering; where I early found
The voice of passion fail in the far reaches,
And youth's hot tumult melt in grateful peace,
I shall abide; the wall of chill reserve
I build more just and firm. Here is no failure,
Rather a clear recall my inmost soul
Sounds, that no further I may tread the steep,
And fall to lot of common humankind.
Like one who travels from a city's bounds,
And sees the lessening lights upon the night,
And the wide circle of his sight grows lone,

But overhead the large-faced moon is calm,
And the great winds are free to utter speech—
The city's tumult left behind, the pain of friendship,
The fierce remorse of love, the belittling sense
That comes of too much intercourse with men,
All these and worser left behind forever—
While the vext heart resumes its nobler peace,
The sea of thought upheaves no more with storm,
And inner weds the outer large repose,
Like him who thus hath found what long he sought,
I wander inward from the wizard sense,
Release me from its many dear deceits,
And rest within the spirit's solitude.
O mighty Thought! O Silence vast, profound!
O region of Ideals still, majestic,
The very temple and the home of Gods,
The atmosphere of causes, and the eagle-nest
Of glorious influences ruling all the worlds,
In you my mind and soul shall ever dwell!
O noblest Truth! to you is dedicate
My mind, my strength, my hope, my all of being,
You take I for my bride, you sole I love,
Upon your altar as a sacrifice
I shed my blood, and sink in worldless rest!

TANTALUS.

THE truth is so; Apollo was my friend,
And I held high acquaintance with the gods,
And sat with them at table in the days
When youth and cheerful spring-time ruled my life.
I saw the mighty Thunderer on his throne,
And fickle Juno laughing at his side;
I saw the lightning of his sudden smile
Fill the far spaces of the Heavens with light,
And from the vantage of my topmost outlook,
I saw its radiance trembling to its fall,
Saw its swift flash across the universe,
And knew that in the realms of all the worlds
New apprehensions changed the face of time.
But chief Apollo was my friend, as dear
To me as mother to her clinging child;
For from the fountains of his gracious power
I drank large draughts of inspiration, felt
That in the embrace of his transcendent love
My being blossomed to its utmost height.
I saw him pass Aurora's golden gates,
And flood with sunshine the yet slumbering world;
I saw his car speed through the spiritual realms,
And rise a sun upon the souls of men,
Or beings likest men in all the worlds.
But why recall those vanished joys of youth?
Here in the depths of Hell I sit and mourn;

Yet I will tell you how it came I fell.
One day the Thunderer, gazing straight at me,
In tones of soft compassion said, "Ah, child,
Too soon thou venturest on celestial plains,
Too little canst thou mould thy budding life
In harmony with the universal laws."
He spoke, and on Apollo's cheek there fell
A tear, and Heaven grew dark with misery.
Men tell a vain and foolish tale of me,
That I revealed the secrets of the gods;
For not with revelations are the gods
At strife, all noble work is revelation,
Inspired of them; but they cannot endure
The impotent efforts of half-witted men,
Of souls who labor in a partial way,
And mar their work with thoughtless zeal, or toil
To give expression to a lofty dream
In ignorance of the tools they needs must use.
Two worlds a man must make his home in; foremost
The world of thought, and then by consequence
The world of sense, where principles grow fact,
And the idea finds expression fit.
Therefore I fell; I drank the nectar, fed
The ambrosia, heard the words of all the gods,
But from the bliss of my abstract ideal
Could not descend, and hear the talk of men,
Nor understand the laws of shop and mart,
Nor join the pleasures of the laboring earth.
Therefore I fell, and hence my punishment:
Within the sea of lofty thoughts I sit,
But of them I can gain nor food nor drink,
And over me there hangs the shuddering doom.

And am I hopeless or despairing? Nay,
I know the unfathomable love of Heaven,
I know the gods are past our finding out,
I know that in their providential care
No woe shall stand unbalanced of its joy.
Already through the gloom of yonder sky,
This moonless night that girds me thick about,
I catch faint gleams of glad returning light;
Already yonder eastern sky empurpling
Quivers as if soft-touched by dawn, and soon
I know Apollo's golden fire will burn
On yonder cloud-rack, and upon my soul
Will rise the morning of eternal day.

PYGMALION.

ONE night beneath the silver silent moon,
While splendent snow-fields gleamed around me lone
And far removed from human neighborhood,
A thought of largest scope flashed on my soul.
The barren trees in dusky solemn lines
Edged the long road, and stood like sentinels
To guard the stillness, or like pillars rude
To hold the dome of cloudless star-sown sky,
And build about the atom, the slight me,
Whose swift pulsations thrilled along my veins,
The spacious church whose lights are moon and stars.
I saw the ages in their ceaseless toil,
And in the opened Heavens I saw sublime
The image of their destinies realized;
I heard the sound of human suffering,
The mingled voices of the periods dead,
The harsh confusion of the time's complaints,
And deep-toned prophecies of woes to come;
But like an under song that through the thrill
And crash of some divinest orchestra
Weaves its slow golden way, and instrument
On instrument absorbs into the flow
Of its all-conquering harmony, I heard,
As in a solemn hush, Pythagoras
Alone beneath the calm Italian night,
The symphony that merges in the swell

Of its unutterable perfectness, all cries,
All sounds, all tones, all words, that clove, that cleave,
Or e'er shall cleave this world-embracing air.
And as the vision faded, and the song
Died in a last burst of its loveliness,
I heard a voice from out the central sky
Speak in the deeps of my entrancéd heart:
"Say thou this vision unto anguished men;
Above the toiling years, beyond all time,
In spaces never mortal eyes beheld,
On shores washed by serenest waves no ship
E'er severed with its sharpened keel, say thou
That in the spiritual plains, the eternal realms,
Firm joyance waits for wisdom-craving man.
Attune thy words unto the vanished tones,
Whose golden splendor sang the perfect world,
The concord of the seasons, and the love
Of star for star, the amity of flower
With sod, the friendship close of man and earth,
The single clue that through the ages runs,
The golden sphere that clips the universe round."
So spake the voice, and so I listening heard;
Then all was still, save through the branches bare
The winds went sobbing like a child in pain,
And all the stars, and their white queen, the moon,
Looked down with thousand eyes of icy dread
Where prone upon the glittering snow I lay.
Slowly I gathered thought and rose and gazed,
And far below the height whereon I stood
In the clear moonlight shone the sleeping town,
And yet beyond the silvered reach of sea.
Therefore I went, and girded up my loins,

And entered on the long unequal strife;
And like a statue, pure and faultless, white,
A woman-form that held my utmost love,
My purpose rose before my growing life,
And ruled my deeds with undisputed sway.
But men received with sneers my burning words,
And laughed to scorn their import, which refused
To clothe its soul of fire in usual forms,
And cloak in shallow nicety of phrase
Its solemn majesty of prophecy.
But for a time I held my soul intact,
Nor soiled with uses base the marble calm
Of my dear love, my statue pedestalled
Within my heart, my spirit's church.
But as the weary years rolled on apace,
And my laborious striving bore no fruit,
My steps grew laggard, and my heart grew cold.
Therefore I thought this high severity,
This tense upholding of a lofty aim,
This lighting beacons on unscalable hills,
This starlike shining inaccessible,
Moves men to laughter, and suffices not.
Men's moods still love the grassy stream-fed fields,
Nor care to breathe the chilly mountain air.
Wherefore I poured my thought in narrower moulds,
And swerved its high significance to meet
The temporary hopes and aims of men.
So round me grew a bitter clamorous sect,
A barking crowd of indurated souls,
Who minced the truth, and looked with hate and scorn
On those who walked without their narrow ring.
Then wealth and luxury played round my feet,

And trumpet-voicéd fame proclaimed my name
In the four quarters of the listening earth.
But in my heart there was a growing blank,
And on my soul, that gazed with longing sore,
The vision visibly darkened day by day.
Wherefore one night in deep despair I went
To the cold summit where the solemn dream
Had visited my unexpectant soul.
And as I clomb the hill, I heard again
The music of the universe, and saw
In gradual clearness the world's destiny,
The universal end that all things serve,
The pure ideal of eternity.
But as I heard, the harmony was snapped,
And fell away in discord, ruinous, harsh,
And as I gazed, the vision shook with earthquake,
Its light endured eclipse, its symmetry
Vanished in waves of chaos dire and vast.
Then round me poured the ocean of that storm,
And in my ears sounded and howled the din
Of winds unearthly making ceaseless moan ;
And then I knew that I was deep in Hell.
One last long look I cast into my heart,
And saw my statue soiled and sensualized,
Bemired, dragged in the dirt of vulgar aims,
Discrowned, and beast in semblance, that shone erst
A woman mild with eyes of love and hope.
Then sunk I depths of Hell unfathomable,
Until I reached this ledge of lingering hope,
Where through the day I weep and pray and weep,
And in the passage of the moonless nights
Sometimes catch sudden gleams of distant stars.

HANGING THE PICTURES.

At last they came, the treasures I had longed
To hold within my hands for many days.
With eagerness I cut the cord and gazed;
From wide unfathomable eyes of bliss
The mystical mother looked upon me there;
The child sat throned upon her arms as King
Of all the worlds and the long reach of time.
I looked at it with feelings gently touched,
And loved the mighty artist for his gift,
Though but a faint reflection was my own.
Now underneath this picture lay one more,
The fair incomparable Madonna, she
Who floats amid the softly-parting clouds,
Her feet upon the moon, and circled by
A crowd of lovely angels, winsome babes,
That take the air as native element,
Miraculous flight of playful birds of Heaven.
I lingered with them long, and gazed at them,
And held them in all lights, and strove to catch
Some glimpse of the deep message they contained.
At length I cut my cord and placed my hooks,
And hung them, but the day was pale and gray,
And rain-clouds strove to weep their bitter tears
For this earth's many sins, and robe in gloom
The habitations and the homes of men.
I could not get them in the proper light,

I took them down and tried another way,
But it was all in vain ; they hung awry,
They were too far apart, they were too near.
I tried again, again, but all in vain.
And now the clouds assembled thick and vast,
The sudden lightning gleamed, and thunder rolled
Sullen across the summer's sultry air.
I sat me down, and could not hold my tears,
And felt somehow an aching sense of loss,
For all my joy was simply dust and ashes.

LYRICAL AND NARRATIVE.

AD POETAM.

What dost thou seek in the night's deep mystery,
   Dreamer of dreams, and singer of songs?
Dost thou believe the world's sad history
     Will cease from its lengthening record of sorrow,
     Will put from itself its grave garment of wrongs,
     Will bask in the light of the sun-mastered morrow,
Because thy keen music dissevers the air,
And all the four winds thy sweet messages bear?

Nay, thou dost say the songs that have gladdened thee
   Sprang from thy heart like young birds from their nest,
Stilled with their murmurs the woes which have saddened thee,
     Rescued thy soul from thy passion's sharp peril,
     Hushed into calm thy tumultuous breast;
     And shall the sweet realm of thy singing prove sterile,
Now thou hast built round the listening heart
A land in whose seasons no winter has part?

Surely with thee, O compassionate singer of songs,
   With thee all is well, O dreamer of dreams;
What though the day, though the night, be the bringer of wrongs,
     Art thou not sovereign of mystical regions,
     Art thou not sovereign of the land which gleams
     With the light of pure Hope's innumerous legions?
Wherefore lead, oh, lead us, to thy realm where spring,
Joy, and clear wisdom abide and sing.

THE NEW MIDAS.

Of old the gracious gods from Heaven descended,
   In hands immortal bearing costly gifts,
With man his daily toilsome pathways wended,
   Shed solemn radiance in transfiguring drifts,
      Radiance of Heaven's midsun,
      On all things thought or done,
With might divine man against men defended,
   From wrong that slays the laboring truth that lifts.

They taught to cleave with prow the unmeasured ocean,
   To harvest wave-ridged fields where foam-flowers grow,
To count Time's all-prevailing pulse and motion,
   The spirit's deepmost mysteries to know,
      To tend the sprouting grain,
      To rear on brown-hued plain
The splendid symbol of the heart's devotion,
   With cities populous the land to sow.

They built much-trodden roads to realms ideal,
   And peopled with their oracles the air,
Uniting in relation hymeneal
   Man's hope and all the fruitful earth did bear,
      So that his visionings
      On splendor-dropping wings
Haunted each vale and glade, and changed the real
   To visible image of his dreams most fair.

Therefore in woods where summer lingered playing,
   Making her footsteps sweet with grass and flower,
Where pleasure circled swart Silenus straying,
   Where Bacchus slept in rose-illumined bower,
      And dryads trod the green,
      And shy soft-eyed were seen
Slim nymphs and oreads going blithe a-Maying,
   Midas, the king, occasion found and hour.

For him, Silenus—who, afar from joyance
   The wine-god's merry crew made in that gloom,
Had wandered, and in bacchant mazed annoyance
   Pondered of satyr lost the imminent doom—
      For guerdon of kind care,
      And conduct safe to where
The grieving master stayed the revel's buoyance,
   Set in the space the glad god's smiles illume.

And Bacchus all King Midas' askings granted,
   Giving him power to change to virgin gold
All things in which his mystic touch implanted
   The virtue magical his hand did hold;
      A shallow boon, indeed,
      Born of material greed,
Of fortunate sequence in due period scanted,
   A fool's desire that scorn and grief unfold.

But, in these latter days, in joys ethereal
   The gods sit on their thrones, forgetting men;
Void is the earth of all their songs imperial,
   Void is each forest deep and rose-clad glen,

  Void is the chainless air,
  Void are the spaces fair
With immemorial march of worlds sidereal,
 Mute are those tones to earthly denizen.

Sometimes sweet companies from the dim spacious
 Plains of the Heavens descend the flushing light,
Circle young hopes with halos warm and gracious,
 Strengthen travailing thought with spiritual might,
  Flit before children's eyes,
  Paint the gold sunrise skies,
Gladden deep-grieving hearts with dreams veracious,
 And cheer brave souls upholding struggling right.

But momentary is the golden vision;
 The level winds upbear not long the feet
Treading secure their waves as fields elysian.
 For one tranced interval the soft wings beat,
  And tones sweet as Love's voice
  Bid the worn soul rejoice,
Then night or daylight stares in grim derision
 On emptied homes and spectre-peopled street.

One god remains man's friend, gold-haired Apollo,
 Mindful of shepherd days when Time was young,
Sad with man's woe, sad with the gladness hollow
 The Fates for world around his soul have hung;
  He knows the burdened heart,
  The clamorous, fruitless part
Of hope bemocked with dream it cannot follow,
 Of mind in anxious dubitation swung.

Therefore, as Bacchus erst in forests olden,
    He gave a gift, but universal, pure;
The gift to change to substance spiritual-golden,
    The shows and forms of all man's life obscure;
        No selfish, thoughtless boon,
        But power to set in tune
The wide world-chaos age on age beholden,
    To build the harmonious sphere that shall perdure.

Therein the passionate sea's deep-throated mystery,
    The high-domed laugh of cloudless mid-day sky,
The light of stars, and weird, unspoken history
    Stream-cloven caves through all their darkness sigh,
        The calms of summit snows
        Flushed with the sunset rose,
And voice of summer's breeze-bent flower consistory,
    Furnish the feast whereby the soul will lie.

Therein the soul in sovereignty pure and regal
    Sceptres the elemental powers at will,
Haunts thought's sea-spaces like a spirit sea-gull,
    Hearkens what songs the empyrean fill,
        Feels through its spirit limbs
        Thrill Love's mysterious hymns,
Spreads its broad wings and soars like sun-born eagle,
    To God's sun-temple crowning God's steep hill.

Therein the nations in firm friendship banded,
    Travelling the centuries loud with rapturous song,
Past the vexed rocks where ancient peoples stranded,
    Secure from war and hatred's poisonous wrong,

One body, one wide heart,
To earth's remotest part,
One great world-giant, conquer Fate, and landed
On greener shores the pastoral times prolong.

Therein the One supreme, the ineffable glory,
The soul of love and substance pure of good,
The infinite might and world-embracing story,
The life of stream and singing-bird and wood,
The trumpet of the storm,
The light whose beams inform
Rapt thought and wisdom with much travail hoary,
Serenely smiles in measureless fatherhood.

O lord Apollo, thee, by night and daytime
Singing we praise and long with thee to be;
Clear as the silver stars at night's mid play-time,
Thou comest that work-wearied men may see;
At autumn's fruitful tide,
By winter's bright fireside,
In rose-draped summer, and in chaster May-time,
We sing the gladness that is still with thee.

THE FEAST OF ROSES.

Argument.—Elagabalus, Emperor of Rome and Priest of the Sun, becoming weary of his Senate, determined to rid himself of them, and at the same time make a sacrifice to his god, the Sun. Wherefore he called them to a sumptuous feast, at which he procured a veritable shower of roses, whereunder they were miserably smothered, and offered up as victims to his refulgent Idol.

How long shall virtue, good, most empty names,
    Bind fast the limbs of him who rules the world?
How long shall senate, state, familiar claims,
    Around his hopes like restless snakes be curled?
How long the power which every pleasure tames
    In virtue's cerements be most basely furled?
Let Love and Joy call forth their happy crowds
Resplendent as a flock of sunset clouds.

From bliss to bliss, the lucent waves of life,
    Let our souls' barques glide onward pauselessly,
Past sound or sight remove all storm and strife,
    Where we seek rest, may calm forever be,
The winds with wildest odors ever rife,
    Mild blossoms grow, and fruits down-load the tree,
Forgotten cares that nest within our hearts,
And slay our dreams with swift envenomed darts.

To-morrow let the all-beholding sun,
    Whose altars smoke with ceaseless sacrifice,
Rejoice as never yet since first begun
    His daily course; his flame-dispersing eyes

Shall dim in smoke of rapturous triumph won,
    For his sake, by the King, who, dust-clad, lies,
Lord of the world, yet abject slave mid slaves,
Before his throne, and his protection craves.

Prepare the feast! To-morrow's noon shall know
    A carnival where life and death shall meet,
Where life in splendor like the sun's shall glow,
    Where death wild revelry shall kiss and greet,
Where joys shall fall like countless flakes of snow,
    Where death shed myriad darts like sharp-tongued sleet.
Sing praises to the Sun, our God, our Lord:
We bring him victims more than war and sword!

Prepare the feast! Earth's choicest treasures spill
    More lavish than the full-blown moon her light;
Bright gold, that filled the bowels of the hill,
    And gems that lay deep-hidden from the sight,
Convert to shapes that suit unfettered will;
    And fruits, and wines that drank immeasured night
Of depths mysterious, flowers, dance, and song,
Our summer tide of revels shall prolong!

At the clear morrow's noon, the palace gates
    Admit the noble, wise, and great, and good;
The regal slendor brightly dissipates
    The latest fear that checked the rapid blood.
Elagabalus, fair amid such mates,
    Reflects on all the radiance of his mood;
Like morn's fair beams traversing a clear lake,
The smiles across his pale face fleet and shake.

Up marble stairs whose balustrades with gold
    Are thick encrusted as the night with stars,
Through halls whose beauty crowns the sense, past old
    Dusk chambers through whose moonlit window-bars
The midnight glow on kingly revels rolled,
    Satiate with splendor that no discord mars,
The dreaming guests follow the rustling girls,
Whose feet make softer music than the whirls

Of midnight oreads in aerial dance.
    Lo! marvels that the brain but half conceives;
For as the darkness flees, when truth's strong lance
    Pierces the air with gleaming strokes and leaves
To light fields uncontested, or as prance
    Morn's radiance-winged coursers, when she weaves
Her night-slaying spell, and showers white floods of splendence
From mane and hoofs across their swift ascendence,

Even thus the night of bliss experienced fled,
    The fiery morn of bliss expectant rose.
Their souls like outworn garments from them shed
    The dreams of the wan past, the real grows
On them as summer's sun on winter dead,
    The fleeting moments novel joys disclose,
Rapture on rapture gradual revel keeps,
Capricious as a fountain's golden leaps.

What mortal tongue may hope in words to tell
    The wonder of the place wherein they stood?
From lands mysterious by some potent spell,
    From sunless depths of seldom-visited wood,

From gloomy cavern or sprite-haunted dell,
  Sprang forth the hands whose subtle masterhood
Fashioned the solid miracle of dream,
Whose wondrous glory did around them gleam.

A vast hall, through whose many-windowed walls
  The noontide fell with yellow fire and flame,
The senses lulled by slumberous water-falls,
  And melancholy strains fitfully came
Like echoes soft and low. Loose-robéd thralls,
  African slaves, like beasts that singers tame,
Recline about the boards of gem-starred gold,
Or in their dusky hands the wine-cups hold.

The roof presents an intertangled net
  Of precious fretwork, vine and grapes and flower,
Around the central orb, all golden, set
  To catch the errant sunbeams, then to shower
A rain of light upon the fount whose wet
  Circumference beneath is bright with dower
Of broad-leaved lilies, round whose thinnest cups
Quick sunbows leap in merry downs and ups.

And myriad loves shoot subtly-pointed darts
  Across the walls, whose crowning carvéd curves
Titans uplift, and on which Painting starts
  Into fair life of thought. Here ocean swerves
As Venus treads its waves like lovers' hearts,
  Here Helen passion's wildest flights ennerves,
Here Phædra spurns the cold Hippolytus,
Here sings of love fierce Sappho amorous.

The tortured earth in meek subservience
   Had oped her thousand doors, and shown her spoils
To countless slaves, who bore her treasures thence,
   And wove them in their unimagined toils
To all that fills the eye, or thrills the sense;
   There lay the fruits and flowers of nameless soils,
The forest and the sea their tribute brought,
Whate'er the brain conceived, the hand had wrought.

The garlands crown the brows, the rosy wine
   Shines thick with sunbeams like weird snakes of fire,
Pleasure and song their passioned souls entwine,
   And wake the slumbering brood of strong desire;
Fiercer the music, wilder wild eyes shine,
   Fiercer the mirth like flames upclambering higher;
Fancy withdraws them from the streaming light,
They live in dreams outshining those of night.

It was the height and fury of the feast;
   The King descends, and through the risen crowd
Walks slow, his priest-garb glorious as the East,
   When morning kindles all its waste of cloud,
Shone in the sun a lesser sun. Sound ceased
   As low a subtle purpose he avowed:
"Ye strove for glory, for the laurel crown,
To-day shall furnish you fair roses of renown."

Like noiseless cloud or breeze he crept away,
   The doors behind him clanged with harshest din;
Wild music rose upon the air. Men say
   A youth whose young years were as thick with sin

As ruins old with ivy, heard that lay
    As he past Circe's isle was wandering.
Fear sprung from sleep that lulled its fiends awhile,
They stood with lifted cup and frozen smile.

Lo! as an exhalation flees the morn,
    The roof recedes before the engulfing air;
They stand amazed, they watch in dread, in scorn,
    The yawning cleft; some sink in weak despair,
Some dream of scenes whose splendor will adorn
    Past splendor; hark! the King's voice low and rare:
"Sing praises to the Sun, our God, our Lord:
We bring him victims more than war or sword!"

Down rang the trembling cups, loud cries of rage
    And fear and woe affright the shaken walls,
The doors are shut. Like tigers in a cage
    They stamp the floor, and beat the space that galls
Their impotence. In vain the white-haired sage,
    The poet, patrician, and most wretched thralls,
Attempt to flee. They wrench the casement bars;
Behold unnumbered spears like midnight's stars.

But, lo! a miracle. The winds are red
    With unimaged rain, that fills the light
With rosy hue like curtains of the bed
    Adonis sleeps on, hid from human sight.
They pause and laugh, mirth is no longer dead,
    They fill the bowl and joy in such a night;
A rain whose drops were roses swiftly fell,
And quick enclosed them in a roseate dell.

They bind the roses in their streaming locks,
    They drink to Joyance, Hope, and mighty Love,
They tear the lilies from the fountain's rocks,
    Their steps to sensuous music nimbly move,
Their blood comes from their hearts in maddening shocks,
    Through dreams their errant fancies errant rove,
And ever fell engirt by odors keen
The roses like a baleful star-shower seen.

Roses, roses, roses, wonderful rain,
    Roses, roses, thicker than wintry hail,
Immixed with blooms that veins of dryads stain,
    And blooms that at a lover's vows grow pale,
White, golden, violet, red, the dim eyes fain
    Would close their weary orbs lest sight should fail;
Roses, roses, roses, ceaselessly falling,
With steps more soft than echo on love faint calling.

Roses, roses, roses, up to the knees,
    Where now lies mirth forgotten and forlorn?
Roses, roses, their fallings do not cease,
    Where now are all the joys that lit the morn?
Roses, roses, roses, their heaps increase,
    Ah! better Death when blows the onset horn.
Roses, roses, roses, up to the neck,
These crowds of their last joy or passion reck.

No breeze disturbs the sky; the risen moon
    Lies in the shivering arms of the dusk east;
The setting sun affrights the eve, at noon
    His rays were paler; like a blood-stained beast

"The King stands on the roof and hearks the tune
   The priests below chant unto their high-priest:
Rejoice! rejoice! O Sun, our God, our Lord,
Thou hast had victims more than war and sword!

ARIADNE.

In the days of the glad, sweet spring of the world,
    In the dewy silver dawn of time,
The flame-wings of legends were loosed and unfurled,
    Those blithe-voiced birds of that clear-ethered clime.

Might I catch the receding tones of those tales,
    And follow the course of their murmurous flow,
Ah, God, to mine eyes would be given the vales
    And the hills whence the sun and the spring never go.

For surely somewhere will the soul find life,
    That thrills through its uttermost fibrils of frame,
With freedom from loss, and trouble, and strife,
    And the far-off fleeting of the loves it would claim.

Of old on the sleep of the brave man there fell
    Dreams clothed about as with fervor of fire,
Fair shapes of dream, with lips sweet from song's well,
    The visible splendor of the soul's chief desire.

So when Theseus lay blind in the prison's night,
    In the dumb, dull stillness no sound broke afar,
Ariadne made flee the darkness like light,
    Shone marvellous-clear on his sight like a star.

And he followed the thread of its golden gleam
    Till the gracious white daylight shone broad on his face,
Past the cowed, crouched monster, out into the stream
    Of the wide, vital air, from the foul, dank place.

And she loved him, clove to him, led him forth,
    Sat with him in his hollow, blue-prowed, swift boat,
Ploughed with him the perilous sea-ways to the north,
    Struck out of his soul its chief pure note.

So the distant and difficult grew near and less hard,
    Compelled by the equable pulse of her breath,
And his spirit waxed clear as the sight of a bard
    Transpiercing the veils of life and of death.

Then the might of the true took hold of him,
    And gave him strong longings for seeing his thought
Take shape and color, from the deepmost dim
    Vast tracts of his soul into body wrought.

So she bade him God-speed, and bade him set sail,
    Lest his love should impede the things to be;
And watched the small speck of his boat sink and fail
    Across the immeasurable glow of the sea.

Ah, brothers, shall our eyes the glad vision rejoice,
    The faultless fair form of the life we would live?
Shall we find outlet from the world's thick noise?
    Has Time the old power such gifts to give?

What has been, shall be; the gods on high
    Sit apart in immutable, happy peace;
They fashioned man and the world; till they die
    Neither pleasure nor pain shall know loss nor increase.

ACTÆON.

Through the green woods the fair morning light
    Flashed in a rain of shattered beams;
Like a frightened thief the swift-winged night
    Fled from the skies with her booty of dreams.

The lucid air of the jocund woods,
    The sense of freedom that filled the green space,
The unseen joys that in numberless broods
    Peopled the dryad-haunted place,

Awoke in the heart of the hunter bold
    The keen desire to follow the game,
And fathom the secret old legends told
    Of a stag that had put all hunters to shame.

He threw his quiver on his shoulder fair,
    He seized his bow in his sinewy hand,
He called to his hounds with a lordly air,
    And felt his breast with his joy expand.

Through the softly-lighted hush of the wood,
    Through the dew-drop's quickly-extinguished shine,
He passed till his lingering footsteps stood
    Before a thicket where the roses' twine

And the envious boughs concealed from sight
    The silver expanse of the secret lake,
Save that sudden gleams like a snow of light
    Burned through the leaf-spaces, fierce flake on flake.

Over his head the sky was blue,
   Around him sounded no living voice;
As he waiting stood the silence grew
   As of one who had lost the power to rejoice.

He knew that the mystery's heart lay bare
   Beyond the green wall's thick-woven screen;
He breathed the entrancéd deep-scented air,
   He halted with troubled and doubtful mien.

A brooding wonder encircled the spot,
   A breathing fear as though one stood
On the verge of the universe, and caught
   A glimpse of the high God's solitude.

His hounds lay crouched in the knee-high grass,
   They quivered and crept to their master's feet;
He trembled and longed and trembled to pass,
   And heard the musical waters beat.

With a passionate cry he sundered in twain
   The hateful leaves that impeded his sight,
And stood transfixed to the spot in pain
   Of a bliss that flooded his soul with light.

Like a statue cut from the moonbeams pale,
   Frozen in all their luminousness,
The goddess stood devoid of veil
   Or garment saving the windy distress

Of her golden hair, that with lambent shine
   Circled her body, and lit with fire
The waters under, where the shadow-leaves twine
   Round her pallid shadow as if sick with desire.

And like lilies that rise on a burnished lake,
   The white-armed maidens, where fancy willed,
Floated, and laughed for Diana's sake,
   As their hollowed palms the water spilled.

Then the goddess turned her cruel pure eyes
   On the bold intruder in a passion of scorn,
And smote with the sword of her grand surprise
   His body through, and his spirit forlorn

Dissevered his loosened limbs' control,
   And shivered the bonds that held him to earth,
As an oak is uptorn when the wind twists the whole
   Of its might round the manifold-ringéd girth.

Like remorseful thoughts that, wakened from sleep,
   Turn on the soul, his maddened hounds
Leaped on their master, and, baying deep,
   Filled with their din the wood's wide bounds.

Deep silence fell on the terrible place,
   Deep silence and darkness of terrible death
On the man who had dared to defile the space
   Where the goddess dwelt with unsanctified breath.

ITHACA.

WEARILY the mariners bend to their toil
    Under the light of the noonday sun ;
Sadly they stoop, and bitterly think
    On the glad days long over and done.

Wastes of pitiless gleaming waves
    Gird them about, and in mocking glee
Rolls and plashes against their keel
    The pauseless jeer of the cruel sea.

Dreams of the distant island home,
    Dreams of wife and questioning child,
Hover before their brooding minds,
    People the air with images mild.

Terrible shores untrodden of men,
    Lying athwart their ways they find,
Infested with beasts, and dreary with moans,
    Making the day beclouded and blind.

Past the perilous charm of the isles
    Sirens encircle with luring song,
They have sailed, heart-drawn to the blooming shores,
    Barely escaping their grievous wrong.

Master, O master, Ulysses wise,
    Lead us beyond the monotonous main ;
Inly we weep, and long to see
    Ithaca's woods and grassy plain.

Ithaca, Ithaca, home of our hearts,
    Shine in the glory of sunset gold!
Shine a soft, rosy cloud in the west,
    Grow on our sight as our way we hold!

Subtly the master smiles with his eyes,
    Points them afar and bids them wait;
Many a time, or ere they return,
    Shall the sun pass his western gate.

Secure in the distance the island lies;
    Surely some day its cloudy shape,
Rising, shall glad their straining gaze,
    Bent on well-loved harbor and cape.

A DREAM.

Across the wide plain of my slumber,
   I saw through shadow and gleam,
The souls of mankind without number
   Proceed in a pauseless stream.

The fount of their coming was hidden
   In a light-suffuséd mist,
And they marched like soldiers bidden
   By a word they could not resist.

They passed into black abysses
   Of a fathomless, moonless night,
Abandoning earthly blisses,
   Forsaking the noonday's light.

African, Chinese, European,
   The several races of man,
Patrician, yeoman, plebeian,
   Swift-changing the river ran.

Each nation upbore a banner,
   Their many wanderings above,
Inscribed in a mystic manner
   With the holy name of Love.

And each passer, though wrinkled and mired,
   Whatever his name or his land,
However equipped or attired,
   Held a fadeless flower in his hand.

And lo! through the darkness before them
   A sudden effulgence glowed,
And I saw beyond them and o'er them
   The end of their toilsome road.

They stood on a plain assembled,
   That glittered with endless spring,
And over them shone and trembled,
   And around them, ring upon ring,

Like an ocean of golden splendor,
   Swept the might of the world's utter Love;
And I saw that this was the sender
   Of all their life from above.

Then the flower each passer had cherished
   Burst forth into lovelier bloom,
And his woes like vapors perished,
   That the ardors of morning consume.

I woke in a joyous shiver,
   And saw through my window-pane
The sun despoiling his quiver,
   And his arrows' golden rain.

THE ROYAL QUESTIONER.

I.

The King said in his heart:
"This is a bitter part
The soul must play
In the resistless sweep and sway
Of mighty powers that build the world.
I sought not life;
Into the strife
Some supreme power hurled
My infant spirit scarcely risen from night.
Now that the light
Of bitter consciousness
Shines on the dire distress,
In whose relentless arms
Perforce I am holden,
I curse the mystic charms
That broke the golden
And dreamless sleep
My soul did keep
Upon the breast of the high God,
Or ere these realms of woe I trod."

II.

The night made no reply;
Across the leaden sky
No star shed radiance pale,
Nor did the moon assail

With motion slow and sweet
The forces of dusk cloud,
Whose outspread crowd
Sometimes make swift retreat,
Sometimes in silver surges beat
Around her lingering feet.
The wind made dreary moan,
And rose and fell in dolorous undertone.

III.

The King said:
"I would that I were dead.
All things I have and hold,
My days are girt with gold;
Like birds from all earth's climes
Swift pleasures fly to me
Uninterruptedly;
The poet in his rhymes
Utters my praises high,
Proclaims my name shall never die,
And writes it like a god's upon the sky;
The beasts of wealth and fame
I long ago did tame;
The wide earth is my slave,
I bind my chains upon the air,
And tread with feet the waters fair;
Yet do I crave
More than all this
To make my sum of bliss.
I cannot see the dream
That comes with vagrant gleam

And shy reserve of its deep loveliness,
A splendid visitant,
Into the drear excess
Of my thought's sad chaotic stress,
I cannot see my dream
Of perfect good,
And justice' utter masterhood,
Pass into life and light,
And scatter wide the cloud of night
Whose despotism
Has cast the nations in the black abysm
Of doubt and fear,
And passion-rulèd cheer.
As some sweet plant
May grow in hidden nook,
By all its sisterhood forsook,
And shed its odor rare
Upon the solitary air,
With no glad eyes to see
Its crescent splendor,
Even so in me
There blooms a tender
And wide-embracing hope,
That right shall cope
With regnant wrong,
And prove more strong.
But all in vain
Are toil and strain;
I strive to find the solemn truth,
I strive to do the supreme good,
But still I fall from lofty mood,
And weep the wasted energies of youth.

My soul is rent in twain,
And seeks to choose in vain
Between the bitter best,
And honey-sweet desire,
That burns like wind-swept fire
Within my breast.
I love all noble things,
But like thin mists at morn
They rise on subtle wings,
And leave my heart in scorn.
This is not life,
This unavailing strife,
This inextinguishable feud
Between myself and good.
Therefore within my heart I said
I would that I were dead."

IV.

The mocking wind,
With voice worn-out and thinned,
Like some old beldam croaking lies,
That bring a pained surprise
Into the maiden's eyes,
Mutters its dismal moan
In the four quarters of the night;
And the wide-wandering tone,
The smothered cry for light,
Pervades the darkling atmosphere.
In gusts of anguish drear
It comes from out the caverns of the east;
Like one who conscience-smitten dies

It comes and falls in broken sighs;
Then, to a shrill woe increased,
It traverses the bounds of space,
And fills each place
With passion sharp and dread,
Till, caught in a strong whirl of sound,
The soul in eddies is tossed round,
And left for dead
In the midst of a sea
Of pain that sighs and sounds eternally.

V.

The King spoke words of scorn:
"The yellow light of morn,
The silence of the dark,
Look on a world of war and hate;
As a stray spark
Of pitiless fire
Oft scatters ruin dire,
And in brief space is strong to dissipate
The high-built domes of weary years,
Even so a drop of strife
Has entered into life,
And poisoned all its several spheres.
In nature's realm
Rude forces overwhelm
The strongly-bastioned fabrics of the ages' toil;
Beast preys on beast,
And gorges on the loathsome feast;
Time wearily makes spoil
Of all its tireless effort strove to build,

And, its long reaches filled
With thick accumulating death,
It laughs in scorn beneath its breath,
And mutters low,
' From overturning unto overturning
My leaden-footed moments go.'
Think on the world of man :
A chaos without plan,
A carnival of passions fierce and rude,
Whose overmastering brood
With savage glee go spurning
Under strong tread
All things for which brave hearts have bled
And poured out life
Upon the fields of strife.
No lofty aspirations
Transfuse with hope the death-chilled nations ;
The mad, ignoble fight for gain,
The dominance of bitter hate,
The wide-spread rule of fear and pain,
The death-in-life of resignation unelate,
The ever-growing forms of ill,
My being fill
With wild despair,
And hatred of the vital air.
There is no God,
Or, if there be,
Treads He no more the earth as once He trod
The far-off fields of Galilee ?
I cannot pierce the storm whose roof
Against the light is solid-proof,
Through might of vapors thick and vast

Heaped up in all the ages past.
I see no way
Into the regions of the day.
I would that I and all this world were drowned
In a still ocean's depths profound,
Past sight or sound,
Where dreamless sleep
In its dumb calm our tumult might forever keep."

VI.

The silence dread
Was as the silence of the dead ;
The wind no longer sought to fill
With prophecies of ill
The vacant realms of space ;
While clouds made bold to interlace
Great gulfs of gloom
With depths of night, dark as the doom
Of souls lost in the trackless wastes of sin.
Without, within,
Throughout the visible sphere,
Throughout the King's tempestuous soul,
Reigned passioned fear,
And uttermost expanse of dole.

VII.

Then spoke a voice
Whose faintest tremble made the heart rejoice ;
A wondrous voice whose tone
Seemed effluent
From nature's inmost element,
As though the world-soul spoke,
And its mysterious silence broke.

It shook the lone
Wide air into a soft, delicious thrill of sound,
That reached the heart's profound,
And lit with hope its lampless bound.
"O tortured one,
Thine anguish has its utmost done.
Dost thou not see
Thy limitless expanse of destiny?
Because within thy soul
There dwells the vision of the whole,
The world's vast scene of violence
Offends thine inner loftier sense.
Thou art the King;
Dost think a slave could bring
Against the All such questioning?
Thy toil and pain
Are only steps to perfect gain;
Within thy heart reside
The pure realities that shall abide,
That rule all spaces and all times,
And bind all chaos in a poet's rhymes.
Within thee find the kingdom sure
That shall endure;
And in the light of joy and hope
Heaven's doors shall ope,
And on thy trancéd sight shall fall
The vision of the Supreme Wisdom, guarding, loving
    all."

VIII.

Then, like a rose
That in a queen's deserted garden blows,

And fills the barren waste
With splendor chaste,
The moon shone in the east;
And, one by one, the stars
Rode into sight upon their viewless cars;
Till the mild glow, increased
To a pale sea of light,
Flooded the night;
And, like faint echoes of some subtle song,
That tenderest memories prolong,
The winds made utterance sweet,
And sped on swiftest feet
Across the air's wide mere,
And utterly displaced the latest shade of fear.

LONGING.

I.

WILL it be, will it be, in the ages to come,
  In the years of our life in other spheres,
When we shall have gathered the whole vast sum
Of suffering, and winnowed the wheat from the chaff?
  Or will the small scope of the years
      We spend on this earth,
      In plenty and dearth,
Wherein we labor and seldom laugh,
Reveal the precious, the priceless boon,
The meaning, the sense of the mystic rune,
Inscribed on our foreheads, engraved on our hearts?

II.

Ah, the earth is old and gray:
In the voice of the night and sound of the day,
In the cry of its deep abysses
And all its wildernesses,
In the howl of jungled beast and hiss of crested snake,
  In the moan of the vast immemorial sea,
    In the sigh of the homeless wind,
In the pitiless fall of the snow, fierce flake by flake,
    In the winter trees like old age pinched and
      thinned,
  In the sobs of all living things that be,

In the tears of the poor in the pestilent city
Over whom the skies shut devoid of pity,
In the whole wide anguish,
Wherein the slow months languish,
That nowhere finds Hope, or Heaven, or God,
But back into the night of fear has trod,—
In the one large toil of the world and the soul,
Do you note the stress of longing?

III.

What is it that we seek?
What is it that we crave?
In the atmosphere chill and bleak—
Wherein we dwell—
Our breathing is hard and slow:
We call on Nature to save;
We strive to burst the spell
That binds us in bonds we deeply know.

IV.

With passion, with might,
We seek the light.
Like the plantlet in the ground,
Like a soul in a swound,
Like a truth expressed in speech,
Like a heart endowed to teach,
Like a poet rudely hurled
In the tumult of the world,
Like a prophet whom men scorn,
Like a world in space new-born,

With passion and with might
We seek the light.

V.

This is the sense of the mystic rune
   Inscribed on our foreheads, engraved on our hearts;
This is the sense of the marvellous tune
   The bent trees sing, when the wild wind parts
The thick-woven clouds that hide the sky;
      The bee in the clover,
      The swift bird-rover
Seeking the climes that warmly lie
   In the sun's straight beam,
The flush of summer, the return of spring,
The sweet new thoughts May and April bring,
   The voice of the loosened stream
When winter has sought his northern lair,
And the earth rejoices in the sunlight fair,
   The growth of grasses, the shinings of stars,
     The interchange of night and day,
   All growth that struggles to burst the bars
     Setting it hinderance and delay,
   All storm, all tumult, that fills the breast,
     Utters the secret as best it may,
Life seeks a beyond, a highest, a best.

VI.

Will it be, will it be,
   Will the sure light shine?—
Behind the veil, beyond the sea,
   Will peace be thine and mine?

VII.

Lo! the stress of longing shall create
That it longs for; bear and wait;
Lo! the ages in their toil and dust
Have not faltered in their trust;
Life shall widen, grow completer,
Passion fainter, labor sweeter;
In the longing see expressed
Promise of the happy rest.
Since the soul is nobler far
Than all things that in time are,
Not in temporal gauds and goods
Can its higher-flying moods
Find the calm it seeks perforce:
Nobler, loftier is its course.
Therefore through all Nature's spheres
Ceaseless longing still appears;
Therefore passion, bitter pain,
Reigns within the soul's domain.

VIII.

Complete is the soul,
It demands the whole;
  Its rest is sure,
  And shall endure.
Through the might of longing it will surely gain
Its dwelling upon the celestial plain;
Clothed in the sun, and robed in the sky,
Knowing nor low nor high,
At the heart of things, in the bosom of God,
Its journeyings will end, all roads overtrod.

WEAVING.

I.

THOU canst not rest;
   All day thou sittest
In a toil most blest;
All the day long thou weavest
Sweet dreams in which thou believest;
   All the day long thou sittest,
   And into the dream thou fittest
Soft color and passionate splendor,
All things most fierce and tender,
All hopes, all faiths, all visions,
The soul's superb derisions
Of futile wrong's misprisions,
Life's uttermost swift pleasures,
And whatso of pure treasures
Is kept for rarest trances,
And fugitive glad glances,
When the mystery unfolds,
And Heaven no farther fastness holds.

II.

   Subtle weaver!
   Fearest thou no deceiver?
Dost hold for true
All thy quick hands may do?

What if thou wake from dreaming,
And find mere shadowy seeming
Thy webs of joy and beauty,
Thy miracles of duty,
Thy mystical clear Heaven,
Thine attendant spirits seven,
Thy God, in whom thou believest,
Who weaves in all thou weavest—
What if a dream
These but seem,
And thou more frail than air,
With thy bliss and despair,
Passest as the night
Flees the light!

III.

Yea, thou weavest on
Till the daylight be gone,
Till the sea have an end,
And the Heavens shall bend,
The bright stars fall
From the blue sky's hall,
Till the winds shall come together
In one burst of mixéd weather,
And fleet away
From the realm of day,
Till the passage of the year
Will no more appear,
The vast web of things
Assume broad wings,
And God and the world
In one ruin be hurled.

IV.

Weave, weave!
Thee no destiny can deceive!
For the King of weavers sits
At the world-loom, and he fits
All thy threads in pattern fine
That can join his wide design.
Weave, weave!
Thee no destiny can deceive!
Thou art but the serving-man,
Doing what thy strong hands can;
But the Master works and dwells
In thy labor, and he tells
Into thine attentive ear
Tales that rid thee of all fear:
   The grace of flowers
   In the summer's bowers,
   The voices that spill
   Sweet songs on meadow and hill,
   The dance of the moon,
   To an unheard tune,
   Through the lustrous crowds
   Of maiden clouds,—
Still the season will return
Having these within her urn;
   The truth of sages,
   And the poet's miraculous pages,
   All deeds of good
   That resound through the solitude
   Of the buried past,
All these are thine:

These will last,
And these will shine;
　For the Supreme Weaver sits
　At the world-loom, and he fits
These into his wide design.
Lo! thy weaving is but his
Love of thy deep ecstasies;
Wherefore fear not, day or night,
Sleep of sleep or sight of sight,
And of all thou dost or art
He is the inner, better part,
Soul of soul, and breath of breath,
And, at last, thy death of death!

MY SHIP.

I.

Whither, oh, whither, my ship, wilt thou go?
  I launch thee upon an invisible sea;
    Through the gloom of dreams
    Where naught is but seems,
Through the realms where the winds of wild hope blow,
Through the chill, clear air and sunlight strong of
    thought,
  Through the land of sure reality,
Through regions of splendor by marvellous hands of
    spirits wrought,
    I watch thy sail
  Across the ocean's broad expanses pass and fail.

II.

From island to island thy swift sails bear thee,
  From continent to continent thy sharp keel glides;
    Where the wild wind abides
In his home of storms, thy gleaming sails declare thee;
  From the sweet green shores of summer lands
Thy passionate joys and longings tear thee,
Till the icy fields of the winter's regions,
Resplendent with shine of innumerous legions
Of sun-touched sparkles of stainless snow,
Engird thee with lambent and languid glow.

III.

Wilt thou not pause and rest,
By the mild winds be caressed
Of a patient love that would bind and hold thee,
In arms of quiet and slumber enfold thee,
Shield thee from pain, and keep thee unoppressed
In its warm storm-shielded nest?
Nay—nay—through the measureless reaches of time,
And boundless changes of possible spaces,
Mutable bliss of mutable climes,
Vagrant joys of mutable places,
Summer and winter and silver spring,
Late autumn when the birds no longer sing,
Passions and splendors and aspirations,
And Pleasure's multitudinous-clothéd nations,
Sorrows, and all the delight they bring,—
Sail, O my ship, sail, O my thought,
Seek what none other has ever sought;
On ways untrod save by royal feet,
On winds for weaklings too rapturous-fleet,
Speed, O my ship;
Linger not where the dull time employs
Sullen labor in sullen joys;
Forth through the ether, my ship, my thought,
Through regions thine own impulses have wrought,
Ceaselessly sail,
Till thou sink and fail
In the heart of sovereign and sunlike God,
In the passionate soul that floods the world,
Till the path thy keel has overtrod
Leads to the light in whose glory hurled

Thou wilt mix, O my thought, with the life that is,
With the supreme bliss of supremest bliss,
  With the strife and the life
  Wherewith the All is rife,
  Till thou wilt be
Conjoined with the sovereign Divinity!

SUCCESS.

I.

He has failed, you say:
From the rise to the set of day
His name is not heard:
He has abandoned his lofty schemes,
He is lost in idle dreams,
The event has not occurred,
His star is not seen in the sky,
There is nothing left him save to die.

II.

Poor fool! in your little world
The all is not done;
Much is finished, much begun
Beyond the circlet of your life.
Since when has the stream been hurled
Of the universal strife
Over your mountain wall
To foam and appall,
Where the peaceful denizens of your vale
Meet each the other with simple all hail?

III.

Nay, if, in all the spheres
That greet your eyes and ears,
No banner uprears
The emblazonment of his name,
How dare you call his labor halt and lame?
He thinks, he lives, he is,
He fulfils the hidden Destinies,
He has chosen the silent part
Held close to Nature's heart,
He breathes the breath of her being,
He sees in the sight of her seeing,
He heeds not the loud applause,
He needs not a herald of his cause.
Prate of your slender successes,
Thrid your conventional wildernesses;
He has passed the farthest portal,
He has dropped the vesture mortal,
He has reached the end
Where Man and Life blend,
The ultimate Height,
Bathed in the World-soul for air and for light.

THE FIELD.

WHAT dost thou think thy field will bear
   In the unknown years to come?
Blossom and fruit most rich and rare,
'Trees where the birds are never dumb?

The tears fell like large drops of rain
   Upon the wasted field;
Dost think thy loss will be sure gain,
Thy tear-sown ground sweet harvest yield?

Or, like the sea's unploughed demesne,
   Burst only into flower
Of windy flash and barren green
At fitful will of the sun's power?

Will from the bitter seed grow fruit
   Sweet as the breath of life?
Or can thy impetuous hope compute
The end of the unending strife?

This is a field wondrous and wide,
   Sown with all human tears;
Hark! how the winds of sorrow gride,
Freighted with sobs and sighing fears.

THE FIELD.

This is the field of human woe,
    Wet with all human tears;
How can the white flower, Joyance, grow
From scattered seed of pains and fears?

Thou standest at the heart of night,
    And Hope, the nightingale,
Has poured adown the dark with might
Her final and impetuous wail.

Now not a sound pervades the air,
    Now not a star recalls
The time when youthful life was fair
Within the golden morning's halls.

Nay, if thou weep, profits it thee?
    Will lifted voices pierce
The iron sky of mystery
That clasps and mocks thine anguish fierce?

Sow thou in tears, let who will reap,
    Make no more questioning:
Perchance if thou the summit steep
Wilt climb, a sudden voice will sing

Songs of consolement in thine ear;
    Nay, but I cannot tell;
My toils to me as dark appear
As thine, ruled by the self-same spell.

Take thou thy burden in strong hands;
    What right hast thou to claim
Luxurious life in summer lands,
And freedom from life's grief and shame?

Is it not better thus to be
   Girt for the noble goal,
Than wrapped in pleasure's minstrelsy,
And ignorant of thine own soul?

What signifies thy little life,
   So that the universe
Proceed in light? What if thy strife
Lead thee from better unto worse?

What signifies thy little life,
   So that the general will
Fulfil itself? What if thy strife
Slay thee or ere thou climb the hill?

Whoso will reap, sow thou in tears,
   Make no more questioning;
Hark! through the night across thy fears
Sweet sudden voices strangely sing.

Perchance the just and best are all,
   Believe what seemeth right,
But stand unshaken as a wall
That scorns the whole sea's angry might!

WILD WIND OF THE NORTH.

Wild wind of the north, grim poet of the dark,
   Weaving your fancies across the night;
I seem to see them, forms gaunt and stark,
   And scenes that shun the cheerful light.

Wild wind of the north, through the branches bare
   Blow with your might till their groanings sound
Like the voice of a soul shut out from air,
   In the cell of some sin unfathomably bound.

Wild wind of the north, under the gray sky
   Where never a star-point flickers or gleams,
I stand and laugh and bid you go by
   With the noise of your manifold homeless streams.

Wild wind of the north, fierce spirit of storm,
   Passion and rage of the heart of things,
Soul of the strength that lusts to deform,
   Father of ruin and scatterings,

Shatter the branches and whirl the sleet,
   Rock the unstable homes of men,
Uproot tall oaks, and tread under feet
   Town and village and denizen.

Wild wind of the north, I fear you naught,
    My souls exults in the storm of your might,
My thought flies far with impulsion caught
    From your impotent cries hurled down the night.

Wild wind of the north, hold the globe in your grasp,
    Furl and unfurl the obedient skies,
But more than the might of your strongest clasp
    Is the weakest of babe-souls uttering cries.

Wild wind of the north, I laugh you to scorn,
    You sleep in my soul like a child at rest,
I know you and bind you, and bid you adorn
    My triumph of visions within my breast.

Wild wind of the north, come rest on my wrist,
    My falcon, my bird, my plaything, my sweet,
Fold your strong wings, be still to be kissed,
    Hush your loud sadness, hither retreat.

Wild wind of the north, a single star
    Conquers the clouds you heaped in hate,
Shines and gladdens, and sends afar
    Her challenging light to your empty state.

THE EVENING STAR.

Ah, star! that bring'st the deep still night,
With shine of silver careless light,
Set far in lone expanse of sky,
With no sweet sister star near by,
Hast thou no dreams that from thy peace
Reach out to gain life's golden fleece?

Art thou content with lonely bliss,
And lofty calm, and thought's cold kiss?
With stormless sphere dim clouds above—
Dim clouds of hope and fear and love—
And all the ills that help make up
The mixéd wine of sad life's cup?

Thy shining knows nor pause nor rest,
Thou seemest glad and unoppressed,
Thou know'st not sorrowing, piteous tears,
Thou seem'st unshaken by dim fears;
But thou art silent as gross stone,
And thy white splendor dwells alone.

Ah, star! what mean these strivings fierce
That shake our sphere, our hearts transpierce?
We fear with thee to climb thy height
Encircled by wide waste of night;
We spurn the soil our feet must press,
Yet quake to gain thy loneliness.

THE DROP.

On the rose a rain-drop lay
   In the shadow by the river,
And afar it saw the bay
   In the sunlight curve and quiver.

Was it happy in its world
   Of cool gloom and pale sweet greenery,
Sheltered from the winds that hurled
   Into woe the bay's dim scenery?

What was day or what was night
   To its faintly-hued seclusion,
While the raptures of fierce light,
   And the winds dared not intrusion?

But the haughty river rose,
   Scornful of the banks that bound it,
And it poured its overflows
   In a weltering waste around it.

Rose and violet and lily pale
   Perished in the wild commotion;
Ah, what eager hopes assail,
   As the drop speeds towards the ocean!

Mixed with all the tides it crept
   To the outer world of joyance,
Where the wild winds whirled and swept,
   Where the fleet waves danced in buoyance.

SNOW-MIST.

THIN, subtle, woven fine,
    Pictures quick dismissed;
Wind-blown, rapid, sober shine,
    Fickle, changing mist.

Round the tree-boles, barren, slim,
    Round the branches bare,
Windy snow-waves sinuous swim,
    Ride the snow-foamed air.

On his gray, sad throne of cloud
    Sits the north wind bold,
Has his frosty claims allowed,
    Rules with wand of cold.

Sifted fine, and still more fine,
    Weaving transient webs,
Images of transient shine,
    Snow-mist flows and ebbs.

Fierce and fiercer blows the wind,
    Sifts, and lifts, and sifts,
Thickens where soft heaps have thinned,
    Scatters ridgéd drifts.

Atom, atom, and wind-life,
    World-scheme on world-scheme,—
Whither tends the pauseless strife,
    Flake and gusty gleam?

THE CLIFF.

In a lonely land,
  Sombre and dread,
A tall cliff reared
  Its giant head.

It was brown and bare,
  But the sunrise glow
Shone from its top
  Like silver snow.

Firm-rooted it was;
  The earthquake's shock,
Or the strong wind's might,
  Moved not the rock.

It seemed as old
  As the primal earth;
No mind could tell
  The date of its birth.

A million storms
  Had thundered in vain;
It seemed to laugh
  At the elements' strain.

The fierce sea foamed
  Around its base,
But no change came over
  Its granite face.

THE CLIFF.

The stars at night
  Looked down in dread,
And dreamed it should be
  When they were dead.

The midsummer sun
  Begirt it with flame;
It stood not more calm
  When the winter came.

But a soft breeze blew,
  And it bore a flower
Plucked from the peace
  Of a lady's bower.

Softer than light,
  Softer than air,
It touched the cliff
  With the blossom fair.

And the mighty rock
  Was shattered apart
From glittering top
  To fathomless heart!

THE ROSE.

The pale blue sky gleams through the opening leaves,
    The shadows play across the ground and air,
The yellow sunlight round leaf-rims retrieves
    Its vanquished splendor where the foliage fair
    Shuts out the grass from its fierce pulse and care.

I hear the silence from my window seat,
    And feel the summer entering my veins,
And know with what strange joys the hour-hearts beat,
    The fervorous hours that dance the fleeting plains
    Where Love has birth and sweetest Joy remains.

I see across the way the maid I love,
    Lissome and shy, a part of summer's might,
A life not fallen below, or risen above,
    The bliss of nature's calm, and golden light,
    A maid at flower-stage, flower-like fair and bright.

I know how nature has sheer joy for core,
    How trees put on their leaves for pure desire
To be and live, how clouds dispart in more
    And more for sweet love's sake, and the sun's fire
    Engirds the world as sounds from some great lyre.

I know the secret of the rose, a flame
    Upon its slender stem, the sun's fire burst
Into a visible thing our hearts can name,
    A fire of love in its fierce father-flame immerst,
The word that love and nature live to frame.

THE STAR.

Star, O star, hast thou a story
    Thy silver beams write
    On the page of the night
Of million-yeared labor, and cycle-old glory?

Star, O star, in thy beams are united
    The flash and the flame,
    From worlds without name,
Of passionate joys and loves unrequited.

Star, O star, when the deep night darkens,
    I watch thee glow,
    And somehow I know
Thy heart in a song my rapt soul hearkens.

RESURGENCE.

This is the time of the year's new birth when leaves and grasses,
Blooms sweet-colored, and winds mild-winged, return in their freshness.
Winter is dead, and all the time of ruin and wailing.
Sweetly smiling, and promising purple delights in the summer,
Joy sets her foot on the earth, and, in answer to her enchantment,
Light comes back to the world in a sunrise warm and golden.
Who refrains from rejoicing, or who remains in bondage
Winter, with mistily-falling snows and ice like iron,
Pitiless forged for us, soul and body? Weary longings
Troubled our hearts for the coming of spring, and life, and the sunlight.
Lo! like a sea miraculous, flooding the land as with laughter,
Comes the dominion of flower, and leaf, and low-bowing grasses.
Surely again returns the dominion of smiles and rejoicings;
Surely back to their fastnesses in the sad spaces of sorrow,
Doubt, and fear, and weeping will flee like snows in the sunshine.

O my heart, will not youth and the bliss of its marvellous visions,
Cloud-shapes fantastic, woven in hours of hope, and
unshadowed
Trustfulness, filling with glory as of suns supernatural
the deep sky
Doming the ancient half-forgotten dreamings—O my
heart, say,
Will they return and reclothe and relume, as with
lustre of blossoms,
All the bleak spaces which sorrow and years, like ice-
girdled winter,
Made in the spirit? Speak, O my heart, canst make
responses
Stilling the clamors that din in thine ears, and noises
of weeping,
Half-suppressed as for shame and the courage of des-
peration?
Seems it all in vain? Nay, useless are dreams and
questioning.
Never returns the past, nor the things having been
which are not;
Never returns the power which turned, like a wand
Mercurial,
Sorceries of pain into weird and mystical enchantments
of pleasure;
Nor the touch, like that fabled of old in the fingers of
Midas,
Potent to spiritualize to golden and lovely resplen-
dence
All the dull shows of the life we spend our breath in
the living.

Take thou the day and the hour; what though the sun
 is hidden,
What though the clouds are weaving their gray and
 gloomy engirdment
For the pale welkin, what though the air is solemn
 and heavy,
Life, and time, and labor remain thee, and, in the
 spring-time,
Swift memorial gleams of the sweet-voiced times which
 return not,
Clouds in flocks o'ertravelling the deep blue concave,
 blossoms,
Birds, and winds, in whose hearts reposes the measureless sunshine.

THE NEW DAY.

Sweet day, that openest fair to sight
With gentle floods of early light,
And calm cool winds that pass and fleet
On softly-stepping viewless feet,
I give my heart up unto thee
And float upon thy glad-waved sea.
Unto what isles of better hope,
What mountain-tops of loftier scope,
What vales of grassy low content
Where life in simplest joy is spent,
What intercourse with flood and rill,
What knowledge of the clouds that fill
With cheerful concourse the blue sky,
What chance to dare, what deed to try,
What poet's fancy to unroll,
What leap to learning's utmost pole,
The point of sight and vantage-ground
From whence all mystery is found
In clearest regulation bound,
What sympathy with nature's heart,
Wilt thou unto my soul impart?
The glassy width of mountain lake,
Wherein the tall trees ever take
Miraculous bath, and while on high
They spread their branches to the sky

And know the secret of the sun,
Yet downward still the images run
And bathe themselves within the realm
Where spirit sits beside the helm,
As man looks forth upon the earth
Yet knows his inner higher worth,
The shapes of leaves that show the stress
Of nature's toiling kindliness,
The shadows woven across the trees,
Imagination's witcheries,
The outer show and symbol glad
Of joys the watchful guardians bade
Be given to poets as their lot,
Dream following dream of the Unforgot,
The century-old shapes of desire
Girt by the glow of wondrous fire,
Wilt thou the secret of all these,
That sound within thine every breeze,
Yea more, the mysteries of the mind
That with each human breath resigned
Into thy keeping, make thy sphere
The fluent home of hope and fear,
Wilt thou endeavor to make plain
Unto me, hearkening every strain
That pulsates from thine east and west
And throbs thy sky's benignant breast?
For I would say some slender part,
Not wholly with quaint rustic art,
But fashion for mankind to hear
One faultless song, one dome uprear,
Of precious sound that crystalline
And pure of stain might glow and shine

Upon the age's restless sea,
So wrought of love's high minstrelsy,
That outpoured love of the after-world
Should keep it safe, nor see it whirled
To dark deeps of oblivion,
Being born of joy and deftly spun
Of the eterne substance of the sun.
Above the body's clamorous weight,
That heavy is with sloth and hate,
I rise into the region glad
Where sweet discourse with thee is had,
The region fine and spiritual,
Where all division is but thrall
To deeper union, and the power
Is seen of love, whence like a flower
Of flowers in manifesting clear
The universe is born, and fear
Perishes like an altar smoke
Against the lofty roof-groins broke.
I see the soul of everything,
And from that vision joy to sing ;
And you, O world, may stand to know
What meanings through my new song flow,
The song upon my lips alit,
Born of clear fire, and bold with it,
A bird not seen yet among men,
A miracle past common ken,
An unconsuming wingéd flame
That from mid-heaven's most purest came,
A rose of birds, a flower of song,
Bird-like and flower-like, strange and strong,
And saying with voice most utter true,

The new in the old, and old in new,
The secret poets have ever sung,
Why the round earth in air is swung,
Why planets glow with borrowed light,
And blossom stars strew all the night,
Why rivers murmur as they go,
And the great winds blow to and fro,
What marvellous motions toss and roll
Within the bounds of boundless soul.
O day, I mix myself with thee,
And in thy freedom, too, am free,
And from my lips I soon shall pour
The throng of words that more and more
May bring all listening hearts to thrill
With passions that their music fill,
And men forget their sore dismay,
Born into glow of the New Day.

BEFORE WINTER.

The ashen-hued November sky
   Makes cheerless all the chilly air;
Upon the walks the dead leaves lie,
   And silence hovers everywhere.

A week ago the happy sun
   Had laughed his way across the blue,
And all the trees a garb had won
   More lovely than the spring-time knew.

Adown the streets a golden fire
   Had leaped from tree to neighboring tree;
A flame as of some deep desire
   Had scaled each bough resistlessly.

The maples here and there had shone
   Like prophets in the glow of speech;
And autumn breezes faintly blown
   Some subtle secret striven to teach.

The harvest had been gathered in,
   A splendid smile had flushed the land,
And hearts strange joyance seemed to win
   By ways they could not understand.

Across old Time's o'erarching sky
    The sunset of the year had spread,
And in its rich and plenteous dye
    A gracious promise we had read.

But now around us moans the wind,
    And through the rustling leaves we go;
Like men with faces pinched and thinned
    Against the sky the bare trees show.

A dim foreboding fills our hearts,
    A sombre frown enrobes the day;
Our numbing fancy sadly parts
    With shapes too briefly bland and gay.

We hear the Winter clank his chain,
    His winds are gathered in the north,
His snows are marshalled on their plain
    Of cloud, intent to sally forth.

Which shall our doubting hearts believe,
    The grievous thoughts this drear wind brings,
Or the sweet thoughts that did receive
    Glad hues from autumn's colorings?

Ah, inmost voices whisper soft,
    October's skies shone not in vain;
The year, its gayer plumage doffed,
    Permits the winter's sober reign.

Beneath these sad vicissitudes
    Some strong reality abides,
That winter's regnance still eludes,
    And into genial spring-time glides.

From state to state the wonder speeds,
   It cannot rest, perforce it grows,
And past its brief eclipses leads
   To times when all its splendor glows.

One summit gained, another looms,
   The wonted strife begins anew;
At intervals, beyond these glooms,
   The home of souls gleams on our view.

NOON.

All night my thoughts in wild commotion tossed,
    And sleep forsook the precincts of my brain;
The question in quick-changing guises crossed
    My soul, with fear and suffering in its train.

The night was dark; nor stars nor moon did shine,
    And loudening winds by fits laughed mockingly;
Ever before my sight the silvery line
    Of some idea seemed in scorn to flee.

With unremitting might I strove to reach
    The thought that held within its scope the truth;
But still I failed, like infants trying speech,
    Or boys essaying tasks beyond their youth.

The waning night brought no increase of rest,
    I clamored for the coming of the morn;
Surely with dawn the storm that shook my breast
    Would calm its anger and allay its scorn.

The ruddy sunrise burned along the east;
    I rose, and sadly watched the growth of light;
The day called men and nature to its feast,
    But I remained imprisoned by the night.

NOON.

Lo! sudden gleams within my darkened soul,
  From sources that I knew not, fell and shone;
Could I but master the elusive whole,
  And call my vanished peace once more my own!

Throughout the morn I struggled hard and well;
  The adversary slowly yielded ground,
And from my soul removed his lessening spell—
  I felt my pain had gained its utmost bound.

The sun seemed slow in climbing the steep sky,
  But step by step attained the wonted height;
The day passed to its throne, and from on high
  In broadening circles dropped and surged the light.

Then flashed on me the kernel of my thought,
  And all my wearied powers fell into tune;
I saw the vision which I long had sought,
  And from the distant towers rang out the noon!

A SUMMER MORNING.

I stand beside the stream,
Whose ripples with the beam
Of morning's Orient splendor shine and flow;
I hear the low, sweet plash,
And watch the small waves dash
Against the banks, on which long grasses grow.

Without a cloud, the sky
Sheds from its calm on high
A benediction on the simple scene;
Across the pasture wide
You see the slow stream glide,
And just beyond the wood's thick garb of green.

A peace past word or thought
Its subtle charm has wrought
On distant cornfields bending in the breeze;
It sounds in the bird's song,
It sways in waves along
The yellow wheat that girds the laborers' knees.

Here, in the open field,
The floods of sunshine yield
A sense of some reality that fills,
With waves on waves of light,
Transcending human sight,
All life that dumbly breathes, or conscious thrills.

A SUMMER MORNING.

      Far off, within the wood,
      Starring its solitude,
Swift gleams of bickering radiance flash and fade;
      The light, through close-meshed leaves,
      Its vagrant beauty weaves
Across the stream that waters wood and glade.

      And now the risen sun,
      Its lofty station won,
Floods with its glory the horizon's bound;
      The wild-flowers bend and laugh,
      The birds more gayly quaff
The waters murmuring on with stilly sound.

      I cannot tell what joy
      Gives all my thoughts employ,
And opens to my soul sweet fields unseen;
      As though the shrouding veil
      That wraps earth's painful tale
Had drawn aside its thickly-woven screen.

      I see, O sun! I see
      The open mystery
Of life and time thine opulence makes more clear;
      O type of that deep peace
      That from its high release
Floods with itself this world of grief and fear!

THE INLET.

I watch the many-colored crowd,
    Passing me on the busy street,
And marvel at the faces proud,
    Or sullen with low-browed defeat.

The blue skies smile upon the earth,
    The winds are with the clouds at play,
And happiness had surely birth
    With sundawn of the perfect day.

I dream of all the secrets hid
    By placid brow or gloomy eye,
As in some rock-built pyramid
    An unknown king or slave may lie.

I feel the beat of every heart,
    And shed the tears tired eyes let fall,
And thrill to know myself a part
    Of griefs that weary, hopes that thrall.

Oh, can it be that my weak soul
    Is but an inlet of the sea,
And knows the outer sweep and roll
    Of tides that forerun Destiny?

If this be dreaming, let me hold
    The dear delusion to my breast;
Let me grow fearless, overbold,
    And dare the noblest and the best.

Children of one sweet mother, heirs
    Of all the hopes that thrill all hearts,
And owners of the mystic wares
    That shine within the spirit's marts,

Masters of space and lords of time,
    Wearers of robes that History wove
In far-off looms of every clime,
    In snow-clad wood or olive-grove,

Each soul instinct with all and each,
    We rise at last unto the height,
Foresaid in strange prophetic speech,
    Whence every darkness melts in light!

THE VOICE OF THE SOUL.

From realms of ether I came,
   In realms of ether I dwelt,
Where souls like a circling flame
   Round the throne of the Mystery melt.

But a darkness on me fell,
   I stooped from my station high,
And the mortal, like a spell,
   Estranged me from the sky.

The light of my shining intense
   Grew dim in its vesture cold,
And my heart's heaven-seeking sense
   Was dead as its girding mould.

I forgot my primal life
   In the dream of my daily toil,
In the noise of my daily strife,
   In the dust of the world's turmoil.

One day the scales dropped from my eyes,
   I remembered my secret of birth;
I knew that I came from the skies,
   And held no kinship with earth.

In this river of time and sense
  I float my allotted span,
I return to the regions whence
  I fell when I became man.

Ennobled and purified,
  Freed from this prison of woe,
I wait for the rising tide,
  I long for the shoreward flow.

With the failing of this faint breath
  I shall be on the primal shore,
In the spiritual lands of Death,
  In the Good for evermore.

THE SIRENS.

Over the mountains, and over the sea,
Wilt thou, oh, wilt thou come with me?
Deep-shadowed groves and meadows green,
Splendors no mortal eye has seen,
Singing and mirth the livelong day,
These shall reward thine adventurous way.

Nay, but thy skies were no longer fair,
Golden thy sun, nor perfumed thine air,
Happy thy blossoms, nor silver thy night,
Glorious thy sea's tumultuous might,
Sunderedst thou me from the hearts that I love
In thy griefless expanse of regions above.

Wilt thou remain a slave to thy pain,
Bound in thy passion's unyielding chain?
What are thy loved ones unto thee,
Sad with the whole of misery?
Flee from the midst of thy fierce distress
To my pleasure's wanton wilderness.

Nay, but the gloom of my bitter past
Over thy skies will be surely cast;
Hast thou the power wholly to part
Self from self, or heart from heart?
Whither thou lead'st me, high or low,
Surely myself must with thee go.

Linger not here, but hearken to me,
Seek thou my realm's extremity;
Wilt thou remain in thy semi-gloom,
Haunted as by a perpetual doom?
Shatter the bonds that encircle thee,
Dare to be grandly, utterly free.

Nay, but thy words are vague as the air,
Trouble me not with thy speeches fair;
Whither I go, my word must be said,
My oak-leaf won, my arrow sped;
What matter gloom and bitter pain?
The end is peace, and that is gain.

FAITH.

TEMPT me no more! I hear thee in the dark,
    Muttering thy words of import dire;
Mine eyes fill up with tears, and hardly mark
    My one star paling all its fire.

What hast thou not ta'en from me? joy and hope,
    And life's last priceless, chiefest gift,
Trust that the world has one o'ermastering scope,
    And suffering's clouds gloom but to lift.

I stand alone beneath the deepening night,
    And hark the circling winds that moan,
And bear afar upon their homeless flight
    All grief's impassioned undertone.

All time's great woe seems poured upon the air,
    The oceaned pain engirds me round;
My heart grows cold within me, and I dare
    Not sink beneath the weight of sound.

My one star pulses pale and ghostly sad
    On the black void that apes the sky;
Will it, too, perish, borne on ways that had
    No pity for my truths most high?

Nay, thou shalt shine though all the splendid host
   Merge in the void that mocks at thee,
A beacon on heaven's barely-outlined coast,
   An island on the storm-swept sea.

O kin to what is deepest in my heart,
   The energy to be and live,
The force that rules all change, and hath no part
   In aught the Night and Death may give,

From thee shall spring strange influences to call
   The light back to each starry shell
That floats across the sight in bond and thrall
   To the base Night's o'erpowering spell.

The stars that woke with laughter of the spring
   Shall re-arise in skies that know
The subtle perfumes Love's sweet bowers shall fling
   From blooms that shine and joys that glow.

Tempt me no more with mutterings of ill!
   I will keep vigil till the rose
Of morning's lucency begins to thrill
   From peak to peak of mountain snows.

I will not lose thee, O my light of light,
   Thou shalt not pass forth of my gaze;
Through thee I will make conquest of the Night,
   And bring the sun back to my days.

Whatso will falter, toward thy glow I spring,
   And know not harm nor bitter scathe;
Whatso slips from me, unto thee I cling,
   And lose not my deep faith in Faith!

THE QUEST.

At the gate of the stately garden
   The young man bravely stands;
Afar 'mid the trees the palace
   Overlooks the circling lands.

At the heart of the world, at the centre,
   Where the pulse of the universe beats,
He stands and he bids them open—
   He is scarred with many defeats.

Behind him he sees the marvels
   Of the untold worlds of space,
Of the myriad forms of living,
   Of the spirit's visible face.

Before him he sees the splendor
   Of the infinite might that creates,
Of the life that upholds and strengthens,
   Of the love that labors and waits.

He stands at the gate in patience,
   He fears not the wardens grim,
He has passed through the trackless forest,
   There is naught can terrify him.

THE QUEST.

Though his head grow white with the ages,
   Though the storm howl round him apace,
Though the night come moonless and starless,
   He never reverses his face.

In the palace the servants are busy,
   They furnish the room for the guest,
For the soul that has travailed and conquered,
   That has ceased not from its quest.

He stands till the gate be opened,
   He knows that the end is sure,
That the Soul of all souls has heard him,
   That the might of his joy shall endure.

FOREVER.

Over the snow I took my way,
Just after golden break of day,
From dreams no tongue can rightly say.

The morning air made me feel glad
As fairy breezes Galahad;
I walked with expectation clad.

The mists around me rolled and curled,
Like waves by a fierce storm upwhirled,
Or thoughts in a wild tumult hurled.

The linkèd clouds hid all the sky,
Save where the sunrise made on high
A splendor you might deem God's eye.

My sight was to the sunrise turned,
Its light within my spirit burned,
My feet the snowy pavement spurned.

Into the light I took my way,
Just after golden break of day,
From dreams no tongue can rightly say.

THE ETERNAL HEIGHTS.

Out of the tyranny of moods we must wander
  Into the land of still, calm thought;
Life is so hard, no one may squander
    Aught of the might whereby is wrought
    The realization with anguish bought.

This is the part of the coward and trembler,
  To whiten whenever the trouble comes;
This is the part of the basest dissembler,
    To falter and quake when the drooped head hums
    With the noise of the enemy's jeering drums.

The scene of life's tasks makes little matter;
  A failure here may be victory there;
But the soul must grow used to the hateful clatter
    Of diverse aims, that fills the air
    Through which we journey to summits fair.

And these shine on in eternal sunlight,
  Though mists obscure them from our view;
They shine in the splendor of the mystical One Light,
    The light of Love, the light of the True;
    Our eyes have seen them when skies were blue.

They shine in the soul; man holds them within him;
  They shine though the outmost be dark and chill;
They seem to beckon as though they would win him
    To climb their sides; all is done if his will
    Swerve him to ascend the utmost hill.

FATE.

Three steps and I reach the door,
    But a whole month rolls between
Since last I stood before
    My shut room's simple scene.

I pause at the door and shrink,
    My hand is at point to turn,
But I stand and dimly think
    Of all I long for and yearn.

My life leaps up to me there,
    The past with its every deed,
And I tremble and hardly dare
    The open mystery to read.

A year and a day and awhile,
    Ay me! there is none escape;
Each thought, each dream, each smile
    Will front me in questioning shape.

I open and see what no eyes
    Save mine have the power to see;
Dead scenes and dead griefs arise,
    Dead follies make mouths at me.

Yea, so: through the dark I peer,
    And shudder away from the door;
Voices once heard I hear,
    Know faces seen long before.

A THOUGHT.

You tremble, you shudder, you wince,
  The trouble is hard to bear,
And Time has no power to convince
  That good is the heart of despair.

You tremble, you shake, you thrill,
  The bliss is too much to bear,
And Time has the power to fill
  Your soul with its secret fair.

Ah, sorrow and bliss are twins,
  And joy is yoke-fellow with care,
And who the sweet former wins
  The weight of the other must bear.

Who feels not pain in its might,
  Can feel not the sweetness rare
Of the hope that fills the night
  With its moon-like lustre fair.

SOLITUDE.

The king sat on his throne,
    Alone, alone.

Without, the sunlight fell
    On hill and dell.

Beside the brooklet strayed
    Lover and maid.

Each bird sang to his mate,
    With spring elate.

The king was sad and cold,
    Though clad in gold.

His heart sank in his breast,
    With woe opprest.

His face was marred with scorn
    Of all things born.

Within his golden halls
    Stood countless thralls.

His frown compelled with awe,
    His word was law.

Without, the seasons came
    With snow and flame.

All life, with changes fleet
    Of sad and sweet,

Sought union with the whole,
    Its far-off goal.

He sat upon his throne,
    Alone, alone.

WARNING.

A word, a look, a deed,
  Each light as breathéd air,
    May bring a sudden fate,
And mystically breed
  The black flower of despair,
    Where rose called rose his mate.

Where erst shone peace, the sun,
  And speech welled from the heart,
    A reckless smile or sigh
Is but well past or done,
  And viewless walls dispart
    Two lives that wail and die.

For souls are lightly set
  Upon the spiritual sky,
    As stars that speed and flame;
And if a shock or let
  Falls on the fair star nigh,
    His fellow feels the shame.

Heed well the poet's song;
  In gardens of the soul
    Breathe delicatest blooms;
Beware to do them wrong,
  Lest thou fulfil the whole
    Air of thy life with glooms.

ECHO.

As the leaves in autumn drear
   Float along the sobbing wind,
As if gathering to the bier
Of the swiftly-dying year,

So my memories gather fast,
   Peopling the pale air of mind,
Dig the graves of the sweet past,
And throw on the mould at last.

Like a dream of the dead night,
   Like a cloud of the wan eve,
Like a wave that shone more bright
For the yellow sun's delight,

Joy on joy has gone to death;
   In the dust I sit and grieve,
And my body murmureth
For the ceasing of its breath.

INVITATION.

WHY art thou sad? thou dost not tell;
    Thou hast strange reason for the dim self-pity
That holds thee as with an inflexible spell,
    And moulds to its gloom thy low-voiced ditty.

Is it that thou dost hear the moan
    That fills with its sorrow eternity's spaces?
Is it that thou hast hearkened the tone
    Of secret despair from life's inmost places?

Nay, wake from thy slumber, come forth into light,
    Where the joyous waves of the wide sea glisten,
And the sounds and the gloom of the sad mother-night
    Disturb not the songs whereunto we listen.

PREMONITION.

Hark! through the night didst thou hear the word
  That rang down the air its terror?
Speak! in the night didst thou fear the word
  That muttered the awful error
    Wherein thou art bound?

Yea! thou hast heard the cry of thy fate,
  Bondsman of woe and of sorrow!
Seek not to know, to fathom the why of thy fate!
  In the sea of the awful to-morrow
    Thou art drowned!—art drowned!

A PLATONIC HYMN.

THE sombre eastern skies
Tremble with dawn's surprise,
The crescent radiance floods the impatient air;
The golden sunrise glow
Rises in overflow
Above the wide-spread fields and waters fair.

The moon low in the west
Sinks downward dispossest,
A pallid film of slowly-waning light;
A few stars linger yet,
Worsted and sore beset,
The remnants of the vanishing vanquished night.

But yonder day-god yields
The air's empurpled fields
To regnance of the star-crowned night in turn,
Possessing but half power,
And giving place and hour
To potencies that dimlier shine and burn.

Not such thy might, O Sun!
Who the mid place hast won
In the intellectual regions clear, serene;
Thy lofty centred throne
Abides thy rule alone,
Plato, who Life's profoundest Life hast seen.

Around thee flash and flame
All those of lesser name
Who have loved the Truth and felt her sacred spell,
Who, in the ideal sphere,
Beyond this realm of fear,
Have tasted waters of her secret well.

The Orient dim and vast
Before thy vision past
With hoary seers and old gigantic gods;
India, mother of lands,
Her mighty gates expands
To thee in her unfathomed periods.

And Egypt, vague and strange,
Unfolds the mystic range
Of all her priests and wonder-workers taught;
No peak remains unclimbed,
No utmost depth unmined
Within the wide-extending reach of Thought.

Into the light at length
Greece stepped in youthful strength,
The nursling of the ægis-bearing, blue-eyed queen;
Wisdom upon her smiled,
And called her darling child,
Favored and loved beyond all realms terrene.

White-haired Parmenides,
Across the tumbling seas
Of Generation's many-changing waste,

Saw shine the mystic One,
From whom all life begun,
And in whose round all things and times are placed.

Pythagoras, the mage,
Transcending clime and age,
Lived pure of stain, one with the Truth sublime;
He knew the dateless date
Of all souls' happy fate,
And Spirit's mastery of the sorcerer, Time.

Socrates, called the Wise,
Within whose kindly eyes
All goodness shone, and through whose conquering wit
Injustice clearly saw
Its self-destroying flaw,
And that the Right, by its own splendor lit,

Is king of worlds and men—
Martyr and denizen
Of that realm glorious, Love, the Seer, controls,
Girt by the reverence meet
Of all the gods, thy seat
Is next the Master's in the world of souls.

Thee all of them surround,
Plato, who passed the bound
Set by the learning of the wise of eld,
Thee for whom very Thought
Revealed its secret, and who sought
The One Ineffable and whose eyes beheld.

   Thy words became the source
   Whence Thought received its course
In ages subsequent and born of thine;
   Great Aristotle knew
   How much from thee he drew,
Pure gold brought from thine inexhausted mine.

   Proclus, the dreamer high,
   Sought thee beyond the sky
To fathom what thy deepest speech contains;
   Plotinus into thee
   Swooned in his ecstasy,
Being rapt unto the far empyreal plains.

   In darkness all was lost,
   And earth was tempest-tost
While thou wert hidden from the face of men;
   Again thy sun arose
   At the strange tempest's close,
And thou wast leader of the van again.

   In Florence thy lost voice
   Once more bade Life rejoice,
The bright Heaven of thy musings oped its doors;
   Once more thy music rang,
   And'the vext heart upsprang
Into the light which from thy pages pours.

   And in these final days
   We have not failed to gaze
Where thy hand points, and thy most wondrous words

Recall us from the deep
Possession by earth's sleep,
And sing to us as very morning's birds.

Yea, birds of Heaven, indeed,
Not born of mortal seed,
And pouring thy swift thought across the years,
Thy swift exalting hope,
That looks beyond the slope
That leads down into this abode of tears.

Honored be thy great name,
Holy, and free from blame,
Thou who hast shone a star unto us all;
Monarch and wise art thou,
Around whose placid brow
The laurelled praises of the ages fall.

TUBEROSE.

I.

FLOWER, that I hold in my hand,
Waxen and white and unwoful,
Perfect with your race's lovely perfection,
Pure as the dream of a child just descended from the heavens,
Chaste as the thought of the maid on whose sight first shines the glow of love's planet,
Trustful as a boy who holds the world in hands of power unrelaxing,
Flower, graceful, lovely,
Lo! I give you to the waves that roll across the ocean's expanses.

II.

I watch you like a star on the waters,
I watch you floating away in the distance;
The ocean gives you reception and dwelling,
The ocean with the sweep of its world-encircling currents,
With its storms and winds,—
Mutable home where all is each and each is other.

III.

You show no signs of terror,
You float to the mid-most whirlpool,
You are made one with the unending streams,

The moon and' stars are reflected in your changed
 bosom,
The measureless winds enfold you with love as a gar-
 ment,
Night and day and time are contained in your embraces,
Clouds emerge from your heart and return,
Life and death are as slender ripples across your cen-
 tral calmness,
Hope and wishing and longing and tumult are over,
Unto the all, your cradle and grave, your father-mother,
You have returned,
O flower transfigured!
O flower having reached your fruition!

A SIGH.

I.

Weary, ah, weary am I;
Scorn not thou this cry of sadness,
Scorn not thou me who bow under many a burden;
See I am weak, and clamor for aid which I find not;
See I would be strong, and find each day new bonds
    engirding me.

II.

Oh, might I say in verses the wonderful clearness,
Freshness, gladness, glory all the wide fields are robed in!
Oh, might I be even as they,
Grateful for rain or for sunshine,
Happy in spring when the grasses softly enclothe them,
Bursting to flower, winsome smiles of their green expanses,
Eyed with the splendor of streams that flow on in joyance,
Laugh in summer to feel in their souls the sunshine,
And are content in the winter to sleep in their icy
    enfoldment.

III.

But peace I find not anywhere;
Change brings fear and trembling deep into my soul;
Would I could gain those heights empyrean
Spirits attain who look through this garment of visions,
Seeing beyond the immutable infinite calm of the soul!

SONNETS.

SUSPIRIA.

WILT thou return, who hast abandoned me,
   Thou whom I long for, thou whom I must love?
   I cast mine eyes unto the skies above,
And see but gloom and clouds that turn and flee;
O moonrise or my sunrise, unto thee
   I pour my longing, and have not thereof
   So much of answer as one plume of dove,
Fallen from swift wing of messenger to be
Bringer of tidings glad and gentle words.
   In all this stillness I sink fast toward Death,
      No bodily ceasing but strange loss of soul;
Wilt thou not come, O Song, and wake the birds
   Within me, answering thy faintest breath,
      And sunwise smite the dark that is my dole?

SUB-CONSCIOUS.

W ET with the last night's rain the wood-pile lies
   Beside the walk. Around the crooked sticks,
   Climbing with manifold coquettish tricks,
A morning-glory vine its antics plies,
And lights with vagrant gleam of green surprise
   The darkness of the earthy-colored wood ;
   And like a self-forgetting thought of good
That mitigates the glare of sinful eyes,
Or like pure longings for release from strife,
   Rare premonitions of the better part,
That rise from deeps below the usual life,
   And send unwonted thrills through some worn heart,
Amid the mouldy wood's fantastic rows
A red and luminous morning-glory glows.

SUNRISE IN WINTER.

From depth of dusky dream I woke, and crossed
   The new-fallen snow; the sunrise splendor burned
   Along the sky, and like an alchemist turned
The many clouds, mild winds had deftly tossed
In shapes fantastical as those the frost
   Graves on the window-pane, to crimsoned gold;
   The changeful rosy mists, soft fold on fold,
Crept, lit with radiance, where my gazing lost
The curving sky; I stood within a vale
   Engirt by shifting hills of glorious mist;
     The morning air was glad with colored light,
     The trees like nuns stood wrapt in cloaks of bright
Chaste snow, and from the chimney rose the pale
   Slow smoke to skies that shone clear amethyst.

FOR PICTURES.

I.

WAR.

The night was black with cloud, as though the smoke
   Of battle had congealed, and risen to roof
   The world with gloom; the lurid moon made proof
Of regnancy won by the dark, and broke
In waves of ghostly light; a shattered oak
   Stood in the foreground, and the sentinel
   Far off upon his height kept guard; a spell
Of horror filled the air as when awoke
The cries of onset and appalled the day;
   The half-extinguished flames of the burned town
   Were barely visible; a soldier's corse
And scattered heaps of shapeless things adown
   The plain appeared; and, riderless, a horse
   Took flight and shrilled its agonizing neigh.

II.

PEACE.

In waves on waves of light the high sun rolled
   Across the mid-noon air; midsummer held
   The breathing land, and from its realm expelled
All shapes of fear; mild quiet, fold on fold,

Enwrapped the spreading scene, and in the gold
  Of summer's sun the grass and trees made joy;
  Soft shadows from tall trees had sweet employ
Upon the light-besprinkled stream; made bold
With bliss, the birds wheeled swift across the air;
  The pastures stretched away to where the corn
Rose tall, the farm-house broke the distance, fair
  And cloud-flecked shone the sky, and glad with scorn
Of dull constraint, the horses tossed their manes,
And all forgot their labors and hard pains.

PROGRESS.

AH, blessedness of work; the aimless mind,
Left to pursue at will its fancies wild,
Returns at length, like some play-wearied child,
Unto its labor's knee, and leaves behind
Its little games, and learns to soothe its blind
Wide longings in the sweet tranquillity
Of limited tasks, whose mild successions wind
In pauseless waves unto the distant sea;
For blank infinity is cold as ice,
    And drear the void of space unsown with stars,
    And dolorous the barren line of shore;
Therefore it was with lover-like device
    This lower world was built, through whose cleft bars
    The limitless sun of Truth shines more and more.

WORLD-SLUMBER.

Two thousand years agone within the manger
   They laid the glorious Child, and through the sorrow
   That clothed the world like air, and grew each morrow
Denser with vaporous wrongs, and horrors, stranger
Than all that went before, soft radiance, ranger
   From realms above, floated, and strove to borrow
   Heaven's fire to cleanse the many-centuried morrow
From deep corroding stains; and thou, dear changer
Of old for new lamps, slept; sweet infant slumber,
   Which dreams of rescued souls fulfilled of lucence,
     Whose slow-drawn breaths counted the whole world's risings
From depths of dull despair, whose smiles did number
   Swift star-dawns on the world's night of recusance,
   And bathed mankind in bliss of its comprisings.

PANDEMOS.

I.

What dim mysterious power holdst thou concealed
  In thy most varying play of smiles and moods?
  What soul dare tread thy marvellous solitudes
Of passionate woes by murmurous utterance healed,
Nor cast his whole life's ordinance repealed
  Before thee, that with hands of utmost power
  Thou mayst regift the reborn soul with dower
Thy vagrant swift imaginations yield?
For life is at thy feet, and craves thy will,
  O love, O lady, sovereign of all lands
Wherein wild pleasure from his horn doth spill
  Sweet flowers, whose odors bind with golden bands;
For none may name thee, yet thou holdst men sure,
And leadst them with unconquerable lure.

II.

Past the pale vales with lowly blossoms set,
  Where slender streams sing thinly-sounding songs,
  We have gone to where the nightingale prolongs
Impassioned cadence, and all vain regret
And hollow-hearted fear, snared in the net
  Of bliss, flutter and perish utterly,
  To where love's ultimate strong ecstasy
New heart and soul in outworn life beget.

Yea, drowned beneath thy golden infinite sea,
  Girt by thy multitude of warring waves,
    Mixed in the flow of thy unceasing streams,
All souls who gain thine inmost sanctuary,
  Dwell in thy measureless expanse of graves,
    Live but as one of thy flame-clothéd dreams.

III.

Black night and sea and the loud-sounding wind
  And voices muttering things ill-understood;
  O night gloom with thine utmost hardihood;
O sea mutter as one who deeply sinned;
O wind with hate inexorably twinned,
  Thy storms tumultuous gather thou apace;
  O voices cry aloud through boundless space
What has befallen; lo! spectres pale and thinned.
  Is this the end? Here by the sullen shore
The dream has faded with the sinking sun.
Is the sweet singing past away and done?
  Shall eyes and smiles play sun and moon no more?
The inarticulate vast roar replies,
And gradual clouds engulf the angry skies.

URANIA.

I.

WHAT silver, tremulous gleams sweep o'er the sea,
   Making the air more glad for drops of light,
   And severing in twain the moody plight
Wherein my soul lay, and in flashing glee
Garmenting the waves' lithesome witchery?
   Not all undone the potence of the night
   Sits in mine eyes, and through my languid sight
So rules the day, that subtly come and flee
Cloud-shadows 'twixt the sun and glowing earth;
   But to the shore long grasses creep and laugh,
Upon the cliffs the green-clad trees make mirth;
   I stand aloof, the summer joyance quaff,
And through my heart unwonted pleasures flow,
As through the land the river's sunrise glow.

II.

What thinkest thou? within the lonely glade
   The dryad dwells and dreams the livelong day
   How leaf by leaf her forest clothes the May
With gold-green gloom and sunbeam-haunted shade;
Upon the sky whose slender clouds have made
   A web miraculous wherewith at play
   The winds have shown their inmost fancies gay,
I read the splendid message which shall fade

No more from my deep heart or Nature's scene;
    O soul of things attained and found at last,
        The love that is the fountain and the source
Whence forests bring their periodic green,
    Whence sunlit clouds upon the winds fly fast,
        And passion gains its undiverted course!

III.

O Love that holdst in sweet embrace
    All forms of life, nor basely clingst to one,
    Or in that one seeing but the centred sun
Reflected, dost in clearest eyes but trace
The lineaments of that Universal Face
    That was or ere the strife of sense begun,
    O Love whose image is most deftly spun
Into the spirit of Life's chiefest grace,
And leadst all feet to Beauty's shrine eterne,
    No longer lured on this or that strange way,
    And in all loves loving but thee alone,
We cease the anguish of all those who yearn,
    Being made part of thyself and finding day
    Which but unto thy worshippers is known.

I.—THE SOUL SPEAKS.

Love is the key; we may not climb the height
   Save the strong heart remains sure guide and friend,
   And, looking past these glooms unto the end,
Expects each pulse the slow approach of light;
For we are weak, and wander in a night
   The wizard senses build, wherein they blend
   Strange flames of joys with splendor-stars that send
Weird glamoury of glow across our sight,
And we are bound in chains most hard to break;
   But in our heart's abyss unfathomable
     The instincts toil of higher hopes and sweet,
And as we climb, led by our loves, we take
   Best hold on truths that in these high realms dwell,
     And life's disclosures guide our eager feet.

II.—THE INTELLECT SPEAKS.

We cannot walk thus lampless; Thought alone
  Can find the clew out from this maze's turns;
  Our faith and love wherewith our body burns
End but in darkness silent as a stone;
For love hath end, and by our sorrow's moan
  Our truths are slain, and our great grieving spurns
  Our past belief, and all our labor earns,
Despite tears shed, and without harvest sown,
No space wherein to lay fore-wearied limbs;
    The light of Life shines but where Thought most pure
      Communes with those fixed idealities
Whose mastery weaves our tumults into hymns
  Of rarest sound, whose empire shall endure
    Till Death lays hands on God's own mysteries.

III.—THE SPIRIT SPEAKS.

NAY, out of conflict must come peace; these twain
   Can wage no war upon whose bitter scorn
   There will not rise a reconciling morn,
Nor may by either either yet be slain.
Lo! in the circle of my hands shall gain
   From each be brought the other's brow to adorn,
   And soothe the pain which severance sharp has borne;
For I of both have need, of both am fain.
Lo! unto Love the light of Thought is given;
   Lo! Thought's pale cheeks grow red with Love's own blood;
     Lo! I who hold them friends in my bright sway;
Through me, through me, the bonds of earth are riven,
   The ship securely sails Life's treacherous flood,
     The sunrise burns of ever-widening day!

FULFILMENT.

This is the secret; no fair blossom blows,
  No cloud sails softly down the sunlit sky,
  No clear dusk-shadowed stream goes sweetly by,
No singer lifts his voice in song that glows,
No sower of all these, unless he sows
  For thee, scatters his seed; yea, all is thine;
  With this wide world enclothéd shalt thou shine;
The morning girds thy brow; the virgin vows
  Of untouched thoughts nod their long plumes for thee,
The dim sad past waits for thy harvest-hand,
  The footless future spreads its sun-path lost;
  On oceans smooth or rough no keel has crossed,
Under star-shine no eyes have seen, through bland
  Plains of new flowerage, see, Fate beckons, see!

DEDICATION.

The moon of memory rises clear
   And fills with radiance all the night;
   I am borne back in wondrous flight
To where the pleasant fields appear
Familiar with the blossoms dear
   To times that pour their splendid light
   Into my very sight of sight,
And reassume the engirding atmosphere.

I stand within the mystic land
   Which spirit builds with all the past
   As elements that can but last,
While unforgotten murmurs bland
Of voices whose deep thoughts expand
   Into the glow with boundaries vast,
   Which hope has led to glories fast
By Heaven's mid purport of ideas grand,

Restore the charm that brought my feet
   To water-springs of old renown,
   And hill-tops on whose grassy crown
White temples shone with lore replete
To assuage the pain of life's deceit,
   Persuade the soul to pause, and down
   The green descent with roses sown
To watch glad garments of the Muses fleet.

DEDICATION.

The solemn majesty of peace
   Surrounds me weary with the roar
   Of life that loudens more and more;
At one brave stroke I find release,
In this calm air all tumults cease,
   Old stars into my vision soar,
   And dreams that once my being bore
Into the yellowing fields of thought's increase

Flash through my brain and heart again;
   All things return unto that spring
   Wherein my hopes began to sing;
I am once more the denizen
Of earlier aspirations, past the ken
   Of dullard hours that hardly bring
   One flower its fading light to fling
On toils that are the plodding lot of men.

And lo! my moon reveals a change,
   Its light grows whiter, nobler far,
   Its lustre sweeps transfigured star
On star into its mighty range;
The night transforms its moated grange
   Into a field with bound and bar
   Where sunrise and the sunset are;
What once was lives, and what is now grows strange.

All the sweet past revives and glows
   Around me with the pristine fire
   Suffusing youth's undimmed desire;
The spring of time before the snows

Of disappointment spoiled the rose
   Of half its petals, and the ire
   Of Destiny built smouldering pyre
For much this barren time no longer knows.

I am again with you, dear friend,
   In lands that see no earthly sun,
   But where the threads of life are spun,
The realm of thought without an end
Or mere beginning, whence gods send
   The influence by whose might is done
   Whatever is by action won
From the sheer dark whose dreamy backgrounds lend

Sight and just strength to noblest deeds;
   Nor are we there alone: I sit
   And hark the cadence of your wit;
I bring my blossoms mixed with weeds,
And thrill while many another leads
   By subtle speech or sacred writ
   To that realm's spaces inly fit
For every instant's many-shifting needs.

O'er fountains Oriental, sacred wells,
   Dim distant flower-producing sods,
   Haunts of gigantic mystic gods,
More wondrous than more recent spells
Evoke in simpler-colored dells,
   You wielded strange diviner's rods,
   And as the waters burst the clods
We drank and fled Earth's narrowing cells.

But chief we trod with one who saw
   Life's self unveiled, the top of thought
   And crown of men, whose spirit wrought,
By being's self-returning law
And Time's successive need to draw
   Help from Greek sources deeply fraught
   With all her highest intellects sought,
In you who were his message without flaw.

Above the world we saw the dance
   Of pure Ideas circling through
   The realm of Godhead, and we knew
How thoughts from hidden thoughts advance,
And touched by your illumining lance
   The darkest ways of hope with dew,
   Which winds of sunlight overblew,
Glittered as gloom receded from its glance.

The deep religions of all Time
   Spoke once again through your clear lips,
   Old poets woke from sad eclipse,
And sang as in their golden prime
Of life eternal, and the clime
   Unreached by keel of mortal ships,
   And light whose glorious ocean clips
Those dreams about with mystic rhyme on rhyme.

Wherever thought was loftiest,
   Wherever oracle was heard
   Pronouncing being's solvent word,
Wherever song was chief and best,

And truth sustained the winnowing test
   Of age-long rigor, where new-stirred
   Wise forecast once again recurred
To those dim sources whence have flowed the blest

Assurances of fervid bard,
   That hope achieves its longings high,
   And tears ascend into the sky,
Part of the domes whose building hard
Prepares the fate propitious-starred,
   Which silences Heart's general sigh,
   Making response to every cry,
And fulness gives to soul however marred,

Wherever bliss with instinct sure
   Led to its mid of permanence,
   The home of souls, from wandering whence
Attainment felt itself secure,
Wherever dwelt the stainless-pure,
   We found you, and the freeing sense
   Of high success warred on the dense
And thickening veil which we perforce endure,

The muddying vesture of decay,
   And that dull garb we trod to dust,
   And knew ourselves as know we must,
Children of Light's unchanging day.
You set our feet upon the way
   Of purposed and unfaltering trust,
   You taught to find the worth which rust
Cannot corrupt nor years confuse its ray.

And others mixed a gentler tone
  With your firm voice of sight and power,
  The woman's gracious height of dower
To see the very truth her own,
To gather blooms to thought unknown,
  Rapt feeling's shy and secret flower,
  To gift the many-pleasured hour
With dreams from God's own fastness hither flown.

My thoughts unto those days revert,
  And mingle with those happier eyes
  Alit with flame of fresh surmise,
That doubt was weak to lame or hurt,
Or fear to change their gaze alert
  From seeing past the yielding skies
  Ideal shapes of light arise
Which Time could neither touch nor disconcert.

I know them as my best of friends,
  And separation cannot dim
  The echo of the mutual hymn,
Wherein as parts, whose mixture wends
To music's beauty-fashioning ends,
  We passed thought's ever-widening rim,
  And the world's face of anguish grim
Saw melt in glow that strength with victory blends.

Alack! the band is not complete,
  For some have trod the ways of Death,
  And know the tale his shut mouth saith;
You watched their slowly-vanishing feet

Into the luminous mists retreat,
    And heard the song below the breath,
    Which deep to deep still uttereth,
Love's silent voice than audible tunes more sweet.

They finished well the course ordained,
    Their eyes beheld before their close
    Heaven's white and wondrous central rose;
They passed from life unvexed, unstained,
And many heights of hope attained;
    The vision of their memory grows
    A dream wherein the far light glows
Of that fair clime that soul has never gained,

Save it has had the hardihood
    To penetrate the secrets hid
    In Truth's sky-cleaving pyramid;
Afar from Error's darkling wood
They clomb the mount, and happy stood,
    Where, from earth's lingering traces rid,
    With gaze that feared not lifted lid
They watched reveal itself the Infinite Good.

    ❦

And we shall meet them as before
    Where through the many-blossomed vale
    Truth flows without surcease or fail;
The robe of radiance which they wore
Shall grow in lustre more and more
    As we awake from the sad tale
    Of Time, and hear Love's nightingale
Lighten the space which once sheer darkness wore.

DEDICATION.

I would my words could reach their ear
   Across the gulf that unto us
   Is Heaven's mid self grown amorous
Of those we held so lief and dear;
If the immortals may but hear
   On heights of life less tenebrous,
   And lit by fires that shake not thus
As stars that guide us tremble, dim, and veer,

I pour my song forth of my soul
   Within the realm where their life is
   To mingle with their ecstasies.
And so take what I give; the whole
Of my adventure has for goal
   To voice a glimpse of mysteries
   That underprop the world, and ease
The heart when inner thunders gloom and roll.

These blossoms frail of scent and hue
   In slender swaying growth have won
   Some light of the unfading sun;
They grew in gardens which you knew,
And precious substance deeply drew
   From showers whose skies were overrun
   By cloud-thoughts deftly made and spun
Of words your plenty overbrimmed and threw

Across our mind's horizon, fair
   With sun that answered your clear spell,
   And flooded river, hill, and dell.
These verses are swift flights that dare

The realm of the serener air;
   I wooed them by the mystic well
   Around whose murmurs subtly dwell
The spirits of the life beyond compare.

These narrow pathways haply lead
   To heights wherefrom the truth is seen,
   Life's luring, nay, compelling queen;
Small, rugged, though they be indeed
And overgrown by many a weed,
   Perchance beneath the shadows green
   Of tall and overarching treen
Some joy may make response to some dim need.

In music's noble-thoughted peace
   We meet though distance' envious bar
   Holds our fain hands asunder far;
In thought's soft-lumined high release
Our strengths abound, our souls increase;
   Time has no might to maim or mar
   With its divisions, since we are
Where tumults of the senses fail and cease.

Truth glows around us; we are one;
   The past, the vanished, all are here;
   The mists of the dream disappear,
The Ideal rises with its sun,
Life ever new yet unbegun
   Receives us in its lofty sphere,
   Whence fixed our hearts shall never veer,
Our journeyings surely overpast and done.

www.ingramcontent.com/pod-product-compliance
Lightning Source LLC
Chambersburg PA
CBHW031824230426
43669CB00009B/1215